MW01031171

The Inverted (Covert) Narcissist Codependent

3rd EDITION

Sam Vaknin

The Author is NOT a Mental Health Professional.
The Author is certified in Counselling Techniques.

Editing and Design:

Lidija Rangelovska

A Narcissus Publications Imprint

Prague & Haifa 2018

To get FREE updates of this book JOIN the Narcissism Study List.
To JOIN, visit our Web sites:
http://www.narcissistic-abuse.com/narclist.html or
http://groups.yahoo.com/group/narcissisticabuse

Visit the Author's Web site   http://www.narcissistic-abuse.com
Facebook   http://www.facebook.com/samvaknin
YouTube channel   http://www.youtube.com/samvaknin

Buy other books and video lectures about pathological narcissism and relationships with abusive narcissists and psychopaths here:

http://www.narcissistic-abuse.com/thebook.html

Buy Kindle books here:

http://www.amazon.com/s/ref=ntt_athr_dp_sr_1?_encoding=UTF8&field-author=Sam%20Vaknin&search-alias=digital-text&sort=relevancerank

C O N T E N T S

Throughout this book click on blue-lettered text to navigate to different chapters
or to access online resources

1. The Inverted (Covert) Narcissist: Narcissist Codependent
2. Codependence and Dependent Personality Disorder
3. Narcissists, Inverted Narcissists and Schizoids
4. Schizoid Personality Disorder
5. Avoidant Personality Disorder
6. Negativistic (Passive-aggressive) Personality Disorder
7. Narcissistic Couples: The Double Reflection
8. False Modesty
9. The Narcissist as a Compulsive Giver
10. The Misanthropic Altruist
11. The Green-eyed Narcissist
12. Shame and Existential Anxiety in Narcissism
13. Abuse: Covert and Overt

Author Bio

The Inverted (Covert) Narcissist (Narcissist-Codependent)

Also called "covert narcissist", inverted narcissist is a co-dependent who depends exclusively on narcissists (narcissist-co-dependent).

The inverted narcissist craves to be in a relationship with a narcissist, regardless of any abuse inflicted on her. She actively seeks relationships with narcissists and only with narcissists, no matter what her (bitter and traumatic) past experience has been. She feels empty and unhappy in relationships with non-narcissists.

The Clinical Picture and Developmental Roots - Opening Remarks

Terminology

Codependents

People who depend on other people for their emotional gratification and the performance of Ego or daily functions. They are needy, demanding, and submissive. They fear abandonment, cling and display immature behaviours in their effort to maintain the "relationship" with their companion or mate upon whom they depend. No matter what abuse is inflicted upon them – they remain in the relationship. By eagerly becoming victims, codependents seek to control their abusers.

See also a description of the Dependent Personality Disorder - or its definition in the Diagnostic and Statistical Manual (DSM-IV-TR, 2000).

Inverted Narcissist are Covert Narcissists

The Inverted Narcissist is a co-dependent who depends exclusively on narcissists (narcissist-co-dependent). If you are living with a narcissist, have a relationship with one, if you are married to one, if you are working with a narcissist, etc. – it does *NOT* mean that you are an inverted narcissist.

To "qualify" as an inverted narcissist, you must *CRAVE* to be in a relationship with a narcissist, regardless of any abuse inflicted on you by him/her. You must *ACTIVELY* seek relationships with narcissists and *ONLY* with narcissists, no matter what your (bitter and traumatic) past experience has been. You must feel *EMPTY* and *UNHAPPY* in relationships with *ANY OTHER* kind of person. Only then, and if you satisfy the other diagnostic criteria of a Dependent Personality Disorder, can you be safely labelled an "inverted narcissist".

Not all covert narcissists are inverted narcissists. But all inverted narcissists are covert ("shy", "fragile") narcissists. They are self-centred, sensitive, vulnerable, and defensive, or hostile, and paranoid. They harbour grandiose fantasies and have a strong sense of entitlement. They tend to exploit other, albeit stealthily and subtly. Covert narcissists are aware of their innate limitations and shortcomings and, therefore, constantly fret and stress over their inability to fulfil their unrealistic dreams and expectations. They avoid recognition, competition, and the limelight for fear of being exposed as frauds or failures. They are ostentatiously modest.

Covert narcissists often feel guilty over and ashamed of their socially-impermissible aggressive urges and desires. Consequently, they are shy and unassertive and intensely self-critical (perfectionist). This inner conflict between an overwhelming sense of worthlessness and a grandiose False Self results in mood and anxiety disorders. They team up with classic narcissists (see below), but, in secret, resent and envy them.

Contrary to misinformation spread by "experts" online, covert narcissists are not cunning and manipulative. Classic narcissists are: they often disguise their true nature effectively, knowingly, and intentionally. They are persistent actors with great thespian skills. Not so the covert narcissist: he suppresses his true nature because he lacks the confidence to assert it. His is not a premeditated choice: can't help but shy away. The covert narcissist is his own worst critic. . Lidija Rangelovska suggests that covert narcissism may develop late in life (during adolescence or even early adulthood) as a reaction to abuse by peers or to social rejection.

Inverted narcissism may be the outcome of arrested narcissistic development: the formation of the False Self is disrupted and incomplete and the inverted narcissist is forced to resort to and depend upon the False Self of another narcissist (her partner) in order to regulate her sense of self-worth.

Counterdependents

Most "classical" (overt) narcissists are counterdependent. Their emotions and needs are buried under "scar tissue" which had formed, coalesced, and hardened during years of one form of abuse or another. Grandiosity, a sense of entitlement, a lack of empathy, and overweening haughtiness usually hide gnawing insecurity and a fluctuating sense of self-worth.

Counterdependents are contumacious (reject and despise authority), fiercely independent, controlling, self-centered, and aggressive. They fear intimacy and are locked into cycles of hesitant approach followed by avoidance of commitment. They are "lone wolves" and bad team players.

Counterdependence is a reaction formation. The counterdependent dreads his own weaknesses. He seeks to overcome them by projecting an image of omnipotence, omniscience, success, self-sufficiency, and superiority.

Introduction

Codependence is an important and integral part of narcissism. Narcissists are either counterdependent or codependent (Inverted).

The DSM-IV-TR uses 9 criteria to define the Narcissistic Personality Disorder (NPD). It is sufficient to show signs of 5 of them to be diagnosed as a narcissist. Thus, theoretically, it is possible to have NPD without being grandiose.

Many researchers (Alexander Lowen, Jeffrey Satinover, Theodore Millon and others) suggested a "taxonomy" of pathological narcissism. They divided narcissists to sub-groups (very much as I did with my somatic versus cerebral narcissist dichotomy).

Lowen, for instance, talks about the "phallic" narcissist versus
others. Satinover and Millon make a very important distinction between narcissists who were
raised by "classically" abusive parents – and those who were raised by doting and smothering
or domineering mothers.

Glenn O. Gabbard in "Psychodynamic Psychiatry in Clinical Practice" [The DSM-IV-TR
Edition. Comments on Cluster B Personality Disorders – Narcissistic. American Psychiatric
Press, Inc., 2000] we find this:

*"…what definitive criteria can be used to differentiate healthy from pathological
narcissism? The time honoured criteria of psychological health – to love and to work – are
only partly useful in answering this question."*

*"An individual's work history may provide little help in making the distinction. Highly
disturbed narcissistic individuals may find extraordinary success in certain professions,
such as big business, the arts, politics, the entertainment industry, athletics and
televangelism field. In some cases, however, narcissistic pathology may be reflected in a
superficial quality to one's professional interests, as though achievement in and
acclaim are more important than mastery of the field itself.*

*Pathological forms of narcissism are more easily identified by the quality of the
individual's relationships.*

*One tragedy affecting these people is their inability to love. Healthy interpersonal
relationships can be recognised by qualities such as empathy and concern for the feelings
of others, a genuine interest in the ideas of others, the ability to tolerate ambivalence in
long-term relationships without giving up, and a capacity to acknowledge one's own
contribution to interpersonal conflicts. People who are characterised by these qualities may
at times use others to gratify their own needs, but the tendency occurs in the broader
context of sensitive interpersonal relatedness rather than as a pervasive style of dealing
with other people. One the other hand, the person with a Narcissistic Personality Disorder
approaches people as objects to be used up and discarded according to his or her needs,
without regard for their feelings.*

*People are not viewed as having a separate existence or as having needs of their own. The
individual with a Narcissistic Personality Disorder frequently ends a relationship after a
short time, usually when the other person begins to make demands stemming from for his
or her own needs. Most importantly, such relationships clearly do not 'work' in terms of
the narcissist's ability to maintain his or her own sense of self-esteem."*

*"…These criteria [the DSM-IV-TR's] identify a certain kind of narcissistic patient –
specifically, the arrogant, boastful, 'noisy' individual who demands to be in the spotlight.
However, they fail to characterise the shy, quietly grandiose, narcissistic individual whose
extreme sensitivity to slights leads to an assiduous avoidance of the spotlight."*

The DSM-III-R alluded to at least two types of narcissists, but the DSM-IV-TR committee
chose to delete this:

*"…included criterion, 'reacts to criticism with feelings of rage, shame, or humiliation
(even not if expressed)' due to lack of 'specificity'."*

Other theoreticians, clinicians and researchers similarly suggested a division between "the oblivious narcissist" (a.k.a. overt) and "the hypervigilant narcissist" (a.k.a. covert).

The Compensatory versus the Classic Narcissist

Another interesting distinction, suggested by Dave Kelly in his excellent PTYPES Web site (http://www.ptypes.com) is between the Compensatory Type NPD and the Classic NPD (described in the DSM-IV-TR).

Here are the Compensatory NPD criteria according to Dave Kelly:

"Personality Types proposes Compensatory Narcissistic Personality Disorder as a pervasive pattern of unstable, covert narcissistic behaviours that derive from an underlying sense of insecurity and weakness rather than from genuine feelings of self-confidence and high self-esteem, beginning by early adulthood and present in a variety of contexts, as indicated by six (or more) of the criteria below.

The basic trait of the Compensatory Narcissistic Personality Type is a pattern of overtly narcissistic behaviours (that) derive from an underlying sense of insecurity and weakness, rather than from genuine feelings of self-confidence and high self-esteem."

The Compensatory Narcissistic Personality Type:

- *Seeks to create an illusion of superiority and to build up an image of high self-worth [Millon];*
- *Strives for recognition and prestige to compensate for the lack of a feeling of self-worth;*
- *May "acquire a deprecatory attitude in which the achievements of others are ridiculed and degraded" [Millon];*
- *Has persistent aspirations for glory and status [Millon];*
- *Has a tendency to exaggerate and boast [Millon];*
- *Is sensitive to how others react to him, watches and listens carefully for critical judgement, and feels slighted by disapproval [Millon];*
- *"Is prone to feel shamed and humiliated and especially (anxious) and vulnerable to the judgements of others" [Millon];*
- *Covers up a sense of inadequacy and deficiency with pseudo-arrogance and pseudo-grandiosity [Millon];*
- *Has a tendency to periodic hypochondria [Forman];*
- *Alternates between feelings of emptiness and deadness and states of excitement and excess energy [Forman];*
- *Entertains fantasies of greatness, constantly striving for perfection, genius, or stardom [Forman];*
- *Has a history of searching for an idealised partner and has an intense need for affirmation and confirmation in relationships [Forman];*
- *Frequently entertains a wishful, exaggerated and unrealistic concept of himself, which he can't possibly measure up to [Reich];*
- *Produces (too quickly) work not up to the level of his abilities because of an overwhelmingly strong need for the immediate gratification of success [Reich];*

- *Is touchy, quick to take offence at the slightest provocation, continually anticipating attack and danger, reacting with anger and fantasies of revenge when he feels himself frustrated in his need for constant admiration [Reich];*
- *Is self-conscious, due to a dependence on approval from others [Reich];*
- *Suffers regularly from repetitive oscillations of self-esteem [Reich];*
- *Seeks to undo feelings of inadequacy by forcing everyone's attention and admiration upon himself [Reich];*
- *May react with self-contempt and depression to the lack of fulfilment of his grandiose expectations [Riso].*

Sources:

Forman, Max. Narcissistic Disorders and the Oedipal Fixations. In Feldstein, J.J. (Ed.), The Annual of Psychoanalysis. Volume IV. New York: International Universities [1976] pp. 65-92.

Millon, Theodore, and Roger D. Davis. Disorders of Personality: DSM-IV and Beyond. 2nd Ed. New York: Wiley, [1996] pp. 411-12.

Reich, Annie, [1986]. Pathological Forms of Self-Esteem Regulation. In Morrison, A. P., (Ed.), Essential Papers on Narcissism. pp. 44-60. Reprint from 1960. Psychoanalytic Study of the Child. Volume 15, pp. 205-32.

Riso, Don Richard. Personality Types: Using the Enneagram for Self-Discovery. Boston: Houghton Mifflin [1987] pp. 102-3.

Speculative Diagnostic Criteria for Compensatory Narcissistic Personality Disorder

A pervasive pattern of self-inflation, pseudo-confidence, exhibitionism, and strivings for prestige, that compensates for feelings of inadequacy and low self-esteem, as indicated by the following:

- *Pseudo-confidence compensating for an underlying condition of insecurity and feelings of helplessness;*
- *Pretentiousness, self-inflation;*
- *Exhibitionism in the pursuit of attention, recognition, and glory;*
- *Strivings for prestige to enhance self-esteem;*
- *Deceitfulness and manipulativeness in the service of maintaining feelings of superiority;*
- *Idealisation in relationships;*
- *Fragmentation of the self: feelings of emptiness and deadness;*
- *A proud, hubristic disposition;*
- *Hypochondriasis;*
- *Substance abuse;*
- *Self-destructiveness.*

Compensatory Narcissistic Personality Disorder corresponds to Ernest Jones' narcissistic "God Complex", Annie Reich's "Compensatory Narcissism", Heinz Kohut's "Narcissistic Personality Disorder", and Theodore Millon's "Compensatory Narcissist".

Millon, Theodore, and Roger D. Davis. Disorders of Personality: DSM-IV and Beyond. 2nd ed. New York: Wiley, 1996. 411-12.

Compare this to the classic type:

Narcissistic Personality Type

The basic trait of the Narcissistic Personality Type is a pattern of grandiosity, need for admiration, and lack of empathy.

The Narcissistic Personality Type:

- Reacts to criticism with feelings of rage, shame, or humiliation;
- Is interpersonally exploitive: takes advantage of others to achieve his own ends;
- Has a grandiose sense of self-importance;
- Believes that his problems are unique and can be understood only by other special people;
- Is preoccupied with fantasies of unlimited success, power, brilliance, beauty, or ideal love;
- Has a sense of entitlement: an unreasonable expectation of especially favourable treatment;
- Requires much attention and admiration of others;
- Lacks empathy: fails to recognise and experience how others feel;
- Is preoccupied with feelings of envy.

This is mainly the DSM-III-R view. Pay attention to the not so subtle changes in the DSM-IV-TR – click here to view them and here for more about pathological narcissism.

The Inverted Narcissist

It is clear that there is, indeed, an hitherto neglected type of narcissist. It is the "self-effacing" or "introverted" narcissist. We call it the Inverted Narcissist (hereinafter: IN). Others call it "narcissist-codependent" or "N-magnet" (which erroneously implies passivity and victimhood). Alan Rappaport suggested the name (and diagnosis) "co-narcissist". All inverted narcissists are also covert narcissists (see the terminology section at the beginning of this article.)

The Inverted Narcissist is a narcissist who, in many respects, is the mirror image of the "classical" narcissist. The psychodynamics of the Inverted Narcissist are not clear, nor are its developmental roots. Perhaps it is the product of an overweening Primary Object or caregiver. Perhaps excessive abuse leads to the repression of even the narcissistic and other defence mechanisms. Perhaps the parents suppress every manifestation of grandiosity (very common in early childhood) and of narcissism – so that the narcissistic defence mechanism is "inverted" and internalised in this unusual form.

These narcissists are self-effacing, sensitive, emotionally fragile, sometimes socially phobic. They derive all their self-esteem and sense of self-worth from the outside (others), are pathologically envious (a transformation of aggression), are likely to intermittently engage in aggressive/violent behaviours, are more emotionally labile than the classic narcissist, etc.

There are, therefore, three "basic" types of narcissists:

1. *The offspring of neglecting parents* – They default to narcissism as the predominant object relation (with themselves as the exclusive love object).
2. *The offspring of doting or domineering parents (often narcissists themselves)* – They internalise their parents' voices in the form of a sadistic, ideal, immature Superego and spend their lives trying to be perfect, omnipotent, omniscient and to be judged "a success" by these parent-images and their later representations and substitutes (authority figures).
3. *The offspring of abusive parents* – They internalise the abusing, demeaning and contemptuous voices and spend their lives in an effort to elicit "counter-voices" from other people and thus to regulate their labile self-esteem and sense of self-worth.

All three types experience recurrent and Sisyphean failures. Shielded by their defence mechanisms, they constantly gauge reality wrongly, their actions and reactions become more and more rigid and the damage inflicted by them on themselves and on others is ever greater.

The narcissistic parent seems to employ a myriad primitive defences in his dealings with his children:

Splitting – Idealising the child and devaluing him in cycles, which reflect the internal dynamics of the parent rather than anything the child does.

Projective Identification – Forcing the child to behave in a way which vindicates the parent's fears regarding himself or herself, his or her self-image and his or her self-worth. This is a particularly powerful and pernicious mechanism. If the narcissist parent fears his own deficiencies ("defects"), vulnerability, perceived weaknesses, susceptibility, gullibility, or emotions – he is likely to force the child to "feel" these rejected and (to him) repulsive emotions, to behave in ways strongly abhorred by the parent, to exhibit character traits the parent strongly rejects in himself.

Projection - The child, in a way, becomes the "trash bin" of the parents' inhibitions, fears, self-loathing, self-contempt, perceived lack of self-worth, sense of inadequacy, rejected traits, repressed emotions, failures and emotional reticence.

Coupled with the parent's treatment of the child as the parent's extension, these psychological defenses totally inhibit the psychological growth and emotional maturation of the child. The child becomes a reflection of the parent, a conduit through which the parent experiences and realises himself for better (hopes, aspirations, ambition, life goals) and for worse (weaknesses, "undesirable" emotions, "negative" traits).

Relationships between such parents and their progeny easily deteriorate to sexual or other modes of abuse because there are no functioning boundaries between them.

It seems that the child's reaction to a narcissistic parent can be either accommodation and assimilation or rejection.

Accommodation and Assimilation

The child accommodates, idealises and internalises (introjects) the narcissistic and abusive Primary Object successfully. This means that the child's "internal voice" is also narcissistic and abusive. The child tries to comply with its directives and with its explicit and perceived wishes.

The child becomes a masterful provider of Narcissistic Supply, a perfect match to the parent's personality, an ideal source, an accommodating, understanding and caring caterer to all the needs, whims, mood swings and cycles of the narcissist. The child learns to endure devaluation and idealisation with equanimity and adapt to the narcissist's world view. The child, in short, becomes the ultimate extension. This is what we call an "inverted narcissist".

We must not neglect the abusive aspect of such a relationship. The narcissistic parent always alternates between idealisation and devaluation of his offspring. The child is likely to internalise the devaluing, abusive, critical, demeaning, berating, diminishing, minimising, upbraiding, chastising voices.

The parent (or caregiver) goes on to survive inside the child-turned-adult (as part of a sadistic and ideal Superego and an unrealistic Ego Ideal). These voices are so powerful that they inhibit even the development of reactive narcissism, the child's typical defence mechanism.

The child-turned-adult keeps looking for narcissists in order to feel whole, alive and wanted. He craves to be treated by a narcissist narcissistically. What others call abuse is, to him or her, familiar territory and constitutes Narcissistic Supply. To the Inverted Narcissist, the classic narcissist is a Source of Supply (primary or secondary) and his narcissistic behaviours constitute Narcissistic Supply. The IN feels dissatisfied, empty and unwanted when not "loved" by a narcissist.

The roles of Primary Source of Narcissistic Supply (PSNS) and Secondary Source of Narcissistic Supply (SSNS) are reversed. To the inverted narcissist, her narcissistic spouse is a Source of **PRIMARY** Narcissistic Supply.

The child can also reject the narcissistic parent rather than accommodate her or him.

Rejection

The child may react to the narcissism of the Primary Object with a peculiar type of rejection. He develops his own narcissistic personality, replete with grandiosity and lack of empathy – but his personality is antithetical to that of the narcissistic parent.

If the parent were a somatic narcissist, the child is likely to grow up to be a cerebral one. If his father prided himself being virtuous, the son turns out sinful. If his narcissistic mother bragged about her frugality, he is bound to profligately flaunt his wealth.

An Attempted DSM Style List of Criteria

It is possible to compose a DSM-IV-TR-like set of criteria for the Inverted Narcissist, using the classic narcissists' as a template. The two are, in many ways, two sides of the same coin, or "the mould and the moulded" - hence the neologisms "mirror narcissist" or "inverted narcissist".

The narcissist tries to merge with an idealised but badly internalised object. He does so by "digesting" the meaningful others in his life and transforming them into extensions of his self. He uses various techniques to achieve this. To the "digested", this is the crux of the harrowing experience called "life with a narcissist".

The "inverted narcissist" (IN), on the other hand, does not attempt, except in fantasy or in dangerous, masochistic sexual practice, to merge with an idealised external object. This is because he so successfully internalised the narcissistic Primary Object to the exclusion of all else. The IN feels ill at ease in his relationships with non-narcissists because it is unconsciously perceived by him to constitute "betrayal", "cheating", an abrogation of the exclusivity clause he has with the narcissistic Primary Object.

This is the big difference between narcissists and their inverted version.

Classic narcissists of all stripes reject the Primary Object in particular (and object relations in general) in favour of a handy substitute: themselves.

Inverted Narcissists accept the (narcissist) Primary Object and internalise it – to the exclusion of all others (unless they are perceived to be faithful renditions, replicas of the narcissistic Primary Object).

Criterion ONE

Possesses a rigid sense of lack of self-worth.

The classic narcissist has a badly regulated sense of self-worth. However this is not conscious. He goes through cycles of self-devaluation (and experiences them as dysphorias).

The IN's sense of self-worth does not fluctuate. It is rather stable – but it is very low. Whereas the narcissist devalues others – the IN devalues himself as an offering, a sacrifice to the narcissist. The IN pre-empts the narcissist by devaluing himself, by actively berating his own achievements, or talents. The IN is exceedingly distressed when singled out because of actual accomplishments or a demonstration of superior skills.

The inverted narcissist is compelled to filter all of her narcissistic needs through the primary narcissist in her life. Independence or personal autonomy are not permitted. The IN feels amplified by the narcissist's running commentary (because nothing can be accomplished by the invert without the approval of a primary narcissist in their lives).

Criterion TWO

Pre-occupied with fantasies of unlimited success, power, brilliance and beauty or of an ideal of love.

This is the same as the DSM-IV-TR criterion for Narcissistic Personality Disorder but, with the IN, it manifests absolutely differently, i.e. the cognitive dissonance is sharper here because the IN is so absolutely and completely convinced of their worthlessness that these fantasies of grandeur are extremely painful "dissonances".

With the narcissist, the dissonance exists on two levels:

Between the unconscious feeling of lack of stable self-worth and the grandiose fantasies

AND between the grandiose fantasies and reality (the Grandiosity Gap).

In comparison, the Inverted Narcissist can only vacillate between lack of self-worth and reality. No grandiosity is permitted, except in dangerous, forbidden fantasy. This shows that the Invert is psychologically incapable of fully realising her inherent potentials without a primary narcissist to filter the praise, adulation or accomplishments through. She must have someone to whom praise can be redirected. The dissonance between the IN's certainty of self-worthlessness and genuine praise that cannot be deflected is likely to emotionally derail the Inverted Narcissist every time.

Criterion THREE

Believes that she is absolutely un-unique and un-special (i.e., worthless and not worthy of merger with the fantasised ideal) and that no one at all could understand her because she is innately unworthy of being understood. The IN becomes very agitated the more one tries to understand her because that also offends against her righteous sense of being properly excluded from the human race.

A sense of worthlessness is typical of many other PDs (as well as the feeling that no one could ever understand them). The narcissist himself endures prolonged periods of self-devaluation, self-deprecation and self-effacement. This is part of the Narcissistic Cycle. In this sense, the inverted narcissist is a partial narcissist. She is permanently fixated in a part of the narcissistic cycle, never to experience its complementary half: the narcissistic grandiosity and sense of entitlement.

The "righteous sense of being properly excluded" comes from the sadistic Superego in concert with the "overbearing, externally reinforced, conscience".

Criterion FOUR

Demands anonymity (in the sense of seeking to remain excluded at all costs) and is intensely irritated and uncomfortable with any attention being paid to her – similar to the Schizoid PD.

Criterion FIVE

Feels that she is undeserving and not entitled.

Feels that she is inferior to others, lacking, insubstantial, unworthy, unlikable, unappealing, unlovable, someone to scorn and dismiss, or to ignore.

Criterion SIX

Is extinguishingly selfless, sacrificial, even unctuous in her interpersonal relationships and avoids the assistance of others at all costs. Can only interact with others when she can be seen to be giving, supportive, and expending an unusual effort to assist.

Some narcissists behave the <u>same way</u> but only as a means to obtain Narcissistic Supply (praise, adulation, affirmation, attention). This must not be confused with the behaviour of the IN.

Criterion SEVEN

Lacks empathy. Is intensely attuned to others' needs, but only in so far as it relates to her own need to perform the required self-sacrifice, which in turn is necessary in order for the IN to obtain her Narcissistic Supply from the primary narcissist.

By contrast, narcissists are never empathic. They are intermittently attuned to others only in order to optimise the extraction of Narcissistic Supply from them.

Criterion EIGHT

Envies others. Cannot conceive of being envied and becomes extremely agitated and uncomfortable if even brought into a situation where comparison might occur. Loathes competition and avoids competition at all costs, if there is any chance of actually winning the competition, or being singled out.

Criterion NINE

Displays extreme shyness, lack of any real relational connections, is publicly self-effacing in the extreme, is internally highly moralistic and critical of others; is a perfectionist and engages in lengthy ritualistic behaviours, which can never be perfectly performed (<u>obsessive-compulsive</u>, though not necessarily to the full extent exhibited in Obsessive-Compulsive Personality Disorder). Notions of being individualistic are anathema.

The Reactive Patterns of the Inverted Narcissist (IN)

The Inverted Narcissist does not suffer from a "milder" form of narcissism. Like the "classic" narcissists, it has degrees and shades. But it is much more rare and the DSM-IV-TR variety is the more prevalent.

The Inverted Narcissist is liable to react with rage whenever threatened, or…

…When envious of other people's achievements, their ability to feel wholeness, happiness, rewards and successes, when her sense of self-worthlessness is diminished by a behaviour, a comment, an event, when her lack of self-worth and voided self-esteem is threatened. Thus, this type of narcissist might surprisingly react violently or wrathfully to **GOOD** things: a kind remark, a mission accomplished, a reward, a compliment, a proposition, or a sexual advance.

…When thinking about the past, when emotions and memories are evoked (usually negative ones) by certain music, a given smell, or sight.

…When her pathological envy leads to an all-pervasive sense of injustice and being discriminated against or deprived by a spiteful world.

…When she comes across stupidity, avarice, dishonesty, bigotry – it is these qualities in herself that all types of narcissists really fear and reject so vehemently in others.

…When she believes that she failed (and she always entertains this belief), that she is imperfect and useless and worthless, a good for nothing half-baked creature.

…When she realises to what extent her inner demons possess her, constrain her life, torment her, deform her and the hopelessness of it all.

When the Inverted Narcissist rages, she becomes verbally and emotionally abusive. She uncannily spots and attacks the vulnerabilities of her target, and mercilessly drives home the poisoned dagger of despair and self-loathing until it infects her adversary.

The calm after such a storm is even eerier, a thundering silence. The Inverted Narcissist regrets her behaviour and admits her feelings while apologising profusely.

The Inverted Narcissist nurtures her negative emotions as yet another weapon of self-destruction and self-defeat. It is from this repressed self-contempt and sadistic self-judgement that the narcissistic rage springs forth.

One important difference between Inverted Narcissists and non-narcissists is that the former are less likely to react with PTSD (Post Traumatic Stress Disorder) following the breakup of their relationships with a their narcissists. They seem to be "desensitised" to narcissists by their early upbringing.

Whereas the reactions of normal people to narcissistic behaviour patterns (and especially to the splitting and projective identification defence mechanisms and to the idealisation devaluation cycles) is shock, profound hurt and disorientation – inverted narcissists show none of the above.

The Life of the Inverted Narcissist

The IN is, usually, exceedingly and painfully shy as a child. Despite this social phobia, his grandiosity (absorbed from the parent) might direct him to seek "limelight" professions and occupations, which involve exposure, competition, "stage fright" and social friction.

The setting can vary from the limited (family) to the expansive (national media) – but, whatever it is, the result is constant conflict and feelings of discomfort, even terror and extreme excitement and thrill ("adrenaline rush"). This is because the IN's grandiosity is "imported" and not fully integrated. It is, therefore, not supportive of his "grandiose" pursuits (as is the case with the narcissist). On the contrary, the IN feels awkward, pitted on the edge of a precipice, contrived, false and misleading, not to say deceitful.

The Inverted Narcissist grows up in a stifling environment, whether it is an orthodox, hyper-religious, collectivist, or traditionalist culture, a monovalent, "black and white", doctrinarian and indoctrinating society – or a family which manifests all the above in a microcosm all its own.

The Inverted Narcissist is cast in a negative (emergent) role within his family. His "negativity" is attributed to her gender, the order of her birth, religious, social, or cultural dictates and commandments, her "character flaws", her relation to a specific person or event, her acts or inaction and so on.

In the words of one such IN:

"In the religious culture I grew up in, women are SO suppressed, their roles are so carefully restricted. They are the representation, in the flesh, of all that is sinful, degrading, of all that is wrong with the world.

These are the negative gender/cultural images that were force fed to us the negative 'otherness' of women, as defined by men, was fed to me. I was so shy, withdrawn, unable to really relate to people at all from as early as I can remember."

The IN is subjected and exposed either to an overbearing, overvalued parent, or to an aloof, detached, emotionally unavailable one – or to both – at an early stage of his life.

"I grew up in the shadow of my father who adored me, put me on a pedestal, told me I could do or be anything I wanted because I was incredibly bright, BUT, he ate me alive, I was his property and an extension of him. I also grew up with the mounting hatred of my narcissist brother who got none of this attention from our father and got no attention from our mother either. My function was to make my father look wonderful in the eyes of all outsiders, the wonderful parent with a genius Wunderkind as his last child, and the only child of the six that he was physically present to raise from the get go. The overvaluation combined with being abjectly ignored or raged at by him when I stepped out of line even the tiniest bit, was enough to warp my personality."

The Invert is prevented from developing full-blown secondary narcissism. The Invert is so heavily preoccupied in his or her pre-school years with satisfying the narcissistic parent, that the traits of grandiosity and self-love, even the need for Narcissistic Supply, remain dormant or repressed.

The Invert simply "knows" that only the narcissistic parent can provide the requisite amount of Narcissistic Supply. The narcissistic parent is so controlling that any attempt to garner praise or adulation from any other source (without the approval of the parent) is severely punished by swift devaluation and even the occasional spanking or abuse (physical, emotional, or sexual).

This is a vital part of the conditioning that gives rise to inverted narcissism. Where the narcissist exhibits grandiosity, the Invert is intensely uncomfortable with personal praise, and wishes to always divert praise away from himself onto his narcissist. This is why the IN can only truly feel anything when she is in a relationship with another narcissist. The IN is conditioned and programmed from the very beginning to be the perfect companion to the narcissist. To feed his Ego, to be purely his extension, to seek only praise and adulation if it brings greater praise and adulation to her narcissist.

The Inverted Narcissist's Survival Guide

- Listen attentively to everything the narcissist says and agree with it all.
  Don't believe a word of it but let it slide as if everything is just fine, business as usual.
- Offer something absolutely unique to the narcissist which they cannot obtain anywhere else.
  Also be prepared to line up future Sources of Primary NS for your narcissist because you will not be *IT* for very long, if at all. If you take over the procuring function for

the narcissist, they become that much more dependent on you which makes it a bit tougher for them to pull their haughty stuff – an inevitability, in any case.

- Be endlessly patient and go way out of your way to be accommodating, thus keeping the Narcissistic Supply flowing liberally, and keeping the peace (relatively speaking).
- Get tremendous personal satisfaction out of endlessly giving. This one may not be attractive to you, but it is a take it or leave it proposition.
- Be absolutely emotionally and financially independent of the narcissist. Take what you need: the excitement and engulfment (i.e., NS) and refuse to get upset or hurt when the narcissist does or says something dumb. Yelling back works really well but should be reserved for special occasions when you fear your narcissist may be on the verge of leaving you; the silent treatment is better as an ordinary response, but it must be devoid of emotional content, more with the air of boredom and "I'll talk to you later, when I am good and ready, and when you are behaving in a more reasonable fashion."
- If your narcissist is cerebral and not interested in having much sex, give yourself ample permission to have sex with other people. Your cerebral narcissist is not indifferent to infidelity so discretion and secrecy is of paramount importance.
- If your narcissist is somatic and you don't mind, join in on group sex encounters but make sure that you choose properly for your narcissist. They are heedless and very undiscriminating in respect of sexual partners and that can get very problematic (sexually Transmitted Diseases blackmail come to mind).
- If you are a "fixer" which most Inverted Narcissists are, focus on fixing situations, preferably before they become "situations". Don't for one moment delude yourself that you can actually fix the narcissist – it simply will not happen. Not because they are being stubborn – they just simply can't be fixed.
- If there is any fixing that can be done, it is to help your narcissist become aware of their condition, and (this is very important) with no negative implications or accusations in the process at all.
  It is like living with a physically handicapped person and being able to discuss, calmly, unemotionally, what the limitations and benefits of the handicap are and how the two of you can work with these factors, rather than trying to change them.
- Finally, and most important of all for the Inverted Narcissist: get to know yourself. What are you getting from the relationship? Are you actually a masochist? Why is this relationship attractive and interesting?
  Define for yourself what good and beneficial things you believe you are receiving in this relationship. Define the things that you find harmful to you. Develop strategies to minimise the harm to yourself.
  Don't expect that you will cognitively be able to reason with the narcissist to change who they are. You may have some limited success in getting your narcissist to tone down on the really harmful behaviours that affect you, which emanate from the unchangeable essence of the narcissist. This can only be accomplished in a very trusting, frank and open relationship.

The Inverted Narcissist can have a reasonably good, long lasting relationship with the narcissist. You must be prepared to give your narcissist a lot of space and leeway.

You don't really exist for them as a fully realised person – no one does. They are not fully realised people so they cannot possibly have the skills, no matter how smart or sexy, to be a complete person in the sense that most adults are complete.

Somatic versus Cerebral Inverted Narcissists (IN)

The Inverted Narcissist is really an erstwhile narcissist internalised by the IN. Inevitably, we are likely to find among the Inverted the same propensities, predilections, preferences and inclinations that we do among proper narcissists.

The cerebral IN is an IN whose source of vicarious Primary Narcissistic Supply lies – through the medium and mediation of a narcissist – in the exercise of his intellectual faculties. A somatic IN would tend to make use of his body, sex, shape or health in trying to secure NS for "her" narcissist.

The Inverted Narcissist feeds on the primary narcissist and this is his Narcissistic Supply. So these two typologies can essentially become a self-supporting, symbiotic system.

In reality though, both the narcissist and the Inverted Narcissist need to be quite well aware of the dynamics of this relationship in order to make it work as a successful long-term arrangement. It might well be that this symbiosis would only work between a cerebral narcissist and a cerebral Invert. The somatic narcissist's incessant sexual dalliances would be far too threatening to the equanimity of the cerebral Invert for there to be much chance of this succeeding, even for a short time.

It would seem that only opposing types of narcissist can get along when two classic narcissists are involved in a couple. It follows, syllogistically, that only identical types of narcissist and inverted narcissist can survive in a couple. In other words: the best, most enduring couples of narcissist and his inverted narcissist mate would involve a somatic narcissist and a somatic IN – or a cerebral narcissist and a cerebral IN.

Coping with Narcissists and Non-Narcissists

The Inverted Narcissist is a person who grew up enthralled by the narcissistic parent. This parent engulfed and subsumed the child's being to such an extent that the child's personality was irrevocably shaped by this immersion, damaged beyond hope of repair. The child was not even able to develop defence mechanisms such as narcissism.

The end result is an Inverted Narcissistic personality. The traits of this personality are primarily evident in the context of romantic relationships. The child was conditioned by the narcissistic parent to only be entitled to feel whole, useful, happy, and productive when the child augmented or mirrored to the parent the parent's False Self. As a result the child is shaped by this engulfment and cannot feel complete in any significant adult relationship unless they are with a narcissist.

The Inverted Narcissist in Relationship with the Narcissist

The Inverted Narcissist is drawn to significant relationships with other narcissists in her adulthood. These relationships are usually spousal primary relationships but can also be friendships with narcissists outside of the primary love relationship.

In a primary relationship, the Inverted Narcissist attempts to re-create the parent-child relationship. The Invert thrives on mirroring to the narcissist his own grandiosity and in so doing the Invert obtains her own Narcissistic Supply (which is the dependence of the narcissist upon the Invert for their Secondary Narcissistic Supply).

The Invert must have this form of relationship with a narcissist in order to feel whole. The Invert goes as far as needed to ensure that the narcissist is happy, cared for, properly adored, as she feels is the narcissist's right. The Invert glorifies and lionizes her narcissist, places him on a pedestal, endures any and all narcissistic devaluation with calm equanimity, impervious to the overt slights of the narcissist.

Narcissistic rage is handled deftly by the Inverted Narcissist. The Invert is exceedingly adept at managing every aspect of her life, tightly controlling all situations, so as to minimise the potential for the inevitable narcissistic rages of his narcissist.

The Invert wishes to be subsumed by the narcissist. The Invert only feels truly loved and alive in this kind of relationship. The invert is loath to abandon her relationships with narcissists. The relationship only ends when the narcissist withdraws completely from the symbiosis. Once the narcissist has determined that the Invert is of no further use, and withholds all Narcissistic Supply from the Invert, only then does the Invert reluctantly move on to another relationship.

The Invert is most likely to equate sexual intimacy with engulfment. This can be easily misread to mean that the Invert is himself or herself a somatic narcissist, but it would be incorrect. The Invert can endure years of minimal sexual contact with their narcissist and still be able to maintain the self-delusion of intimacy and engulfment. The Invert finds a myriad of other ways to "merge" with the narcissist, becoming intimately, though only in support roles, involved with the narcissist's business, career, or any other activity where the Invert can feel that they are needed by the narcissist and indispensable.

The Invert is an expert at doling out Narcissistic Supply and even goes as far as procuring Primary Narcissistic Supply for their narcissist (even where this means finding another lover for the narcissist, or participating in group sex with the narcissist).

Usually though, the Invert seems most attracted to the cerebral narcissist and finds him easier to manage than the somatic narcissist. The cerebral narcissist is disinterested in sex and this makes life considerably easier for the Invert, i.e., the Invert is less likely to "lose" their cerebral narcissist to another primary partner. A somatic narcissist may be prone to changing partners with greater frequency or wish to have no partner, preferring to have multiple, casual sexual relationships of no apparent depth which never last very long.

The Invert regards relationships with narcissists as the only true and legitimate form of primary relationship. The Invert is capable of having primary relationships with non-narcissists. But without the engulfment and the drama, the Invert feels unneeded, unwanted and emotionally uninvolved.

When Can a Classic Narcissist Become an Inverted Narcissist?

The rule of thumb is: inverted narcissists act as codependent or inverted when they are paired with a classic narcissist and they act as classic narcissists when they team up with a codependent.

A classic narcissist can become an inverted narcissist in one (or more) of the following (typically cumulative) circumstances:

a. Immediately following a life crisis and a narcissistic injury (divorce, devastating financial loss, death of a parent, or a child, imprisonment, loss of social status and, in general, any other narcissistic injury).
b. When the injured narcissist then meets another - classic - narcissist who restores a sense of meaning and superiority (uniqueness) to his life. The injured narcissist derives Narcissistic Supply vicariously, by proxy, through the "dominant" narcissist.
c. As part of an effort to secure a particularly desired Source of Narcissistic Supply. The conversion from classic to inverted narcissism serves to foster an attachment (bonding) between the narcissist and his source. When the narcissist judges that the source is his and can be taken for granted, he reverts to his former, classically narcissistic self.
   Such a "conversion" is always temporary. It does not last and the narcissist reverts to his "default" or dominant state.

When Can an Inverted Narcissist become a *Classic Narcissist*?

The inverted narcissist can become a classic narcissist in one (or more) of the following (typically cumulative) circumstances:

a. Immediately following a life crisis that involves the incapacitation or dysfunction of the inverted narcissist's partner (sickness, accident, demotion, divorce, devastating financial loss, death of a parent, or a child, imprisonment, loss of social status and, in general, any other narcissistic injury). The narcissistic defences of the Inverted Narcissist and his narcissistic style flare up in reaction to narcissistic injuries and major traumas.
b. When the inverted narcissist, injured and disillusioned, then meets another - inverted - narcissist who restores a sense of meaning and superiority (uniqueness) to his life. The injured narcissist derives Narcissistic Supply from the inverted narcissist.
c. As part of an effort to secure a particularly desired Source of Narcissistic Supply. The conversion from inverted to classic narcissism serves to foster an attachment (bonding) between the narcissist and his source. When the narcissist judges that the source is his and can be taken for granted, he reverts to his former, inverted narcissistic self. Such a "conversion" is always temporary. It does not last and the narcissist reverts to his "default" or dominant state.

Relationships between the Inverted Narcissist and Non-Narcissists

The Inverted Narcissist can maintain relationships outside of the symbiotic primary relationship with a narcissist. But the Invert does not "feel" loved because she finds the non-narcissist not "engulfing" or not "exciting". Thus, the Invert tends to devalue their non-narcissistic primary partner as less worthy of the Inverts' love and attention.

The Invert may be able to sustain a relationship with a non-narcissist by finding other narcissistic symbiotic relationships outside of this primary relationship. The Invert may, for instance, have a narcissistic friend or lover, to whom he pays extraordinary attention, ignoring the real needs of the non-narcissistic partner.

Consequently, the only semi-stable primary relationship between the Invert and the non-narcissist occurs where the non-narcissist is very easy going, emotionally secure and not needing much from the Invert at all by way of time, energy or commitment to activities requiring the involvement of both parties. In a relationship with this kind of non-narcissist, the Invert may become a workaholic or very involved in outside activities that exclude the non-narcissist spouse.

It appears that the Inverted Narcissist in a relationship with a non-narcissist is behaviourally indistinguishable from a true narcissist. The only important exception is that the Invert does not rage at his non-narcissist partner – she instead withdraws from the relationship even further. This passive-aggressive reaction has been noted, though, with narcissists as well.

Inverted and Other Atypical / Partial (NOS) Narcissists

Inverted Narcissists Talk about Themselves

Competition and (Pathological) Envy

"I have a dynamic that comes up with every single person I get close to, where I feel extremely competitive toward and envious of the other person. But I don't ACT competitive, because at the very outset, I see myself as the loser in the competition. I would never dream of trying to beat the other person, because I know deep in my heart that they would win and I would be utterly humiliated. There are fewer things on earth that feel worse to me than losing a contest and having the other person gloat over me, especially if they know how much I cared about not losing. This is one thing that I actually feel violent about. I guess I tend to project the grandiosity part of the NPD package onto the other person rather than on a False Ego of my own. So most of the time I'm stuck in a state of deep resentment and envy toward her. To me, she's always far more intelligent, likable, popular, talented, self-confident, emotionally developed, morally good, and attractive than I am. And I really hate her for that, and feel humiliated by it. So it's incredibly hard for me to feel happy for this person when she has a success, because I'm overcome with humiliation about myself. This has ruined many a close relationship. I tend to get this way about one person at a time, usually the person who is playing the role of 'my better half', best friends or lovers/partners. So it's not like I'm unable to be happy for anyone, ever, or that I envy every person I meet. I don't get obsessed with how rich or beautiful movie stars are or anything like that. It only gets projected onto this partner-person, the person I'm depending on the most in terms of supplies (attention, reassurance, security, building up my self-esteem, etc.)…

…The really destructive thing that happens is, I see her grandiose traits as giving her the power to have anything and anyone she wants. So I feel a basic insecurity, because why should she stay with a loser like me, when she's obviously so out of my league? So really, what I'm envious of is the power that all that talent, social ability, beauty, etc., gives her to have CHOICES – the choice to stay or leave me. Whereas I am utterly dependent on her. It's this emotional inequality that I find so humiliating."

"I agree with the inverted narcissist designation – sometimes I've called myself a 'closet narcissist'. That is, I've internalised the value system of grandiosity, but have not applied the grandiose identity to myself.

I believe I SHOULD BE those grandiose things, but at the same time, I know I'm not and I'm miserable about it. So people don't think of me as having an inflated Ego – and indeed I don't – but scratch the surface, and you'll find all these inflated expectations. I mean to say that perhaps the parents suppressed every manifestation of grandiosity (very common in early childhood) and of narcissism – so that the defence mechanism that narcissism is was 'inverted' and internalised in this unusual form."

"Maybe there aren't two discrete states (NPD vs. 'regular' low self-esteem) – maybe it's more of a continuum. And maybe it's just the degree and depth of the problem that distinguishes one from the other.

My therapist describes NPD as 'the inability to love oneself'. As she defines it, the 'narcissistic wound' is a deep wounding of the sense of self, the image of oneself. That doesn't mean that other disorders – or for that matter, other life stressors – can't also cause low self-esteem. But I think NPD IS low self-esteem…

That's what the disorder is really about – an image of yourself that is profoundly negative, and the inability to attain a normal and healthy self-image…"

"Yes, I'm a survivor of child abuse. But remember that not all abuse is alike. There are different kinds of abuse, and different effects. My XXX's style of abuse had to do with trying to annihilate me as a separate person. It also had to do with the need to put all his negative self-image onto me – to see in me what he hated in himself. So I got to play the role of the loser that he secretly feared he was. I was flipped back and forth in those roles – sometimes I'd be a Source of NS for him, and other times I was the receptacle of all his pain and rage. Sometimes my successes were used to reflect back on him, to show off to the rest of the family. Other times, my successes were threatening to my father, who suddenly feared that I was superior to him and had to be squelched. I experience emotions that most people I know don't feel. Or maybe they do feel them, but to far less extreme intensity. For example, the envy and comparison/competition I feel toward others. I guess most of us have experienced rivalry, jealousy, being compared to others. Most of us have felt envy at another's success. Yet most people I know seem able to overcome those feelings to some extent, to be able to function normally. In a competition, for example, they may be driven to do their best so they can win. For me, the fear of losing and being humiliated is so intense that I avoid competition completely. I am terrified of showing people that I care about doing well, because it's so shaming for me if I lose. So I underachieve and pretend I don't care. Most people I know may envy another person's good luck or success, but it doesn't prevent them from also being happy for them and supporting them. But for me, when I'm in a competitive dynamic with someone, I can't hear about any of their successes, or compliments they've received, etc. I don't even like to see the person doing good things, like bringing Thanksgiving leftovers to the sick old guy next door, because those things make me feel inferior for not thinking of doing that myself (and not having anyone in my life that I'd do that for). It's just so incredibly painful for me to see evidence of the other person's good qualities, because it immediately brings up my feeling of inferiority. I can't even stand to date someone, who looks really good, because I'm jealous of their good looks! So this deep and obsessive envy has destroyed my joy in other people. All the things about other people that I love and take pleasure in is a double-edged sword because I also hate them for it, for having those good qualities (while, presumably, I don't). I don't know – do you think this is garden-variety low self-esteem? I know plenty of people who suffer from lack of confidence, from timidity, social awkwardness, hatred of their body, feeling unlovable, etc. But they don't have this kind of hostile, corrosive resentment of

another person for being all the wonderful things that they can'[...]
etc. And one thing I hate is when people are judgemental of me [...]
can help it. It's like, 'You shouldn't be so selfish, you should feel
successful', etc. They don't understand that I would love to feel th[...]
can't stop the incredible pain that explodes in me when these feeli[...]
often can't even HIDE the feelings. It's just so overwhelming. I fee[...]
There's more, but that's the crux of it for me, anyway."

Getting Compliments

"I love getting compliments and rewards, and do not react negatively to them. In some
moods, when my self-hate has gotten triggered, I can sometimes get to places where I'm
inconsolable, because I get stuck in bitterness and self-pity, and so I doubt the sincerity or the
reliability of the good thing that someone is saying to me (to try to cheer me up or whatever).
But, if I'm in a reasonable mood and someone offers me something good, I'm all too happy to
accept it! I don't have a stake in staying miserable."

The Partiality of the Condition

"I do agree that it's (atypical or inverted narcissism) not MILDER. But how I see it is that it's
PARTIAL. The part that's there is just as destructive as it is in the typical narcissist. But there
are parts missing from that total, full-blown disorder – and I see that as healthy, actually. I see
it as parts of myself that WEREN'T infected by the pathology, that are still intact.

In my case, I did not develop the overweening Ego part of the disorder. So in a sense, what
you have with me is the naked pathology, with no covering: no suaveness, no charm, no
charisma, no confidence, no persuasiveness, but also no excuses, no lies, no justifications for
my feelings. Just the ugly self-hate, for all to see. And the self-hate part is just as bad as it is
with a full-blown narcissist, so again, it's not milder.

But because I don't have the denial part of the disorder, I have a lot more insight, a lot more
motivation to do something about my problems (i.e., I 'self-refer' to therapy), and therefore, I
think, a lot more hope of getting better than people whose defence involves totally denying
they even have a problem."

"When my full-blown XXX's pathological envy would get triggered, he would respond by
putting down the person he was envious of – or by putting down the accomplishment itself,
or whatever good stuff the other person had. He'd trivialise it, or outright contradict it, or find
some way to convince the other person (often me) that the thing they're feeling good about
isn't real, or isn't worthwhile, or is somehow bad, etc. He could do this because the inflated
Ego defence was fully formed and operating with him.

When MY pathological envy gets triggered, I will be bluntly honest about it. I'll say
something self-pitying, such as: 'You always get the good stuff, and I get nothing'; 'You're so
much better than I'; 'People like you better – you have good social skills and I'm a jerk'; and
so on. Or I might even get hostile and sarcastic: 'Well, it must be nice to have so many people
worshipping you, isn't it?' I don't try to convince myself that the other person's success isn't
real or worthwhile, etc. Instead, I'm totally flooded with the pain of feeling utterly inferior
and worthless – and there's no way for me to convince myself or anyone else otherwise. I'm
not saying that the things I say are pleasant to hear – and it is still manipulative of me to say

er person's attention is drawn away from their joy and onto my pain and
ead of doubting their success's worth or reality, they feel guilty about it, or
bout it, because it hurts me so much. So from the other person's point of view,
ot any easier to live with a partial narcissist than with a full-blown, in that their
d successes lead to pain in both cases. It's certainly not easier for me, being flooded
n rage and pain instead of being able to hide behind a delusion of grandeur. But from my
therapist's point of view, I'm much better off because I know I'm unhappy – it's in my face all
the time. So I'm motivated to work on it and change it. And time has borne her words out.
Over the past several years that I've worked on this issue, I have changed a great deal in how
I deal with it. Now when the envy gets triggered, I don't feel so entwined with the other
person – I recognise that it's my OWN pain getting triggered, not something they are doing to
me. And so I can acknowledge the pain in a more responsible way, taking ownership of it by
saying, 'The jealousy feelings are getting triggered again, and I'm feeling worthless and
inferior. Can you reassure me that I'm not?' That's a lot better than making some snide,
hostile, or self-pitying comment that puts the other person on the defensive or makes them
feel guilty… I do prefer the term 'partial' because that's what it feels like to me. It's like a
building that's partially built – the house of narcissism. For me, the structure is there, but not
the outside, so you can see inside the skeleton to all the junk that's inside. It's the same junk
that's inside a full-blown narcissist, but their building is completed, so you can't see inside.
Their building is a fortress, and it's almost impossible to bring it down. My defences aren't as
strong … which makes my life more difficult in some ways because I REALLY feel my pain.
But it also means that the house can be brought down more easily, and the junk inside
cleaned out…"

Thinking about the Past and the World

"I don't usually get rageful about the past. I feel sort of emotionally cut-off from the past,
actually. I remember events very clearly, but usually can't remember the feelings. When I do
remember the feelings, my reaction is usually one of sadness, and sometimes of relief that I
can get back in touch with my past. But not rage. All my rage seems to get displaced on the
current people in my life."

"…When I see someone being really socially awkward and geeky, passive-aggressive,
indirect and victim-like, it does trigger anger in me because I identify with that person and I
don't want to. I try to put my negative feelings onto them, to see that person as the jerk, not
me – that's what a narcissist does, after all. But for me it doesn't completely work because I
know, consciously, what I'm trying to do. And ultimately, I'm not kidding anyone, least of all
myself."

Self-Pity and Depression

"More self-pity and depression here – not so much rage. One of the things that triggers my
rage more than anything else is the inability to control another person, the inability to
dominate them and force my reality on them. I feel impotent, humiliated, forced back on my
empty self. Part of what I'm feeling here is envy: that person who can't be controlled clearly
has a self and I don't, and I just hate them for it. But it's also a power struggle – I want to get
Narcissistic Supply by being in control and on top and having the other person submissive
and compliant…"

Regretting, Admitting Mistakes

"I regret my behaviour horribly, and I DO admit my feelings. I am also able, in the aftermath, to have empathy for the feelings of the person I've hurt, and I'm horribly sad about it, and ashamed of myself. It's as though I'd been possessed by a demon, acted out all this abusive horrible stuff, and then, after the departure of the demon, I'm back in my right mind and it's like, 'What have I DONE???' I don't mean I'm not responsible for what I did (i.e., a demon made me do it). But when I'm triggered, I have no empathy – I can only see my projection onto that person, as a huge threat to me, someone who must be demolished. But when my head clears, I see that person's pain, hurt, fear – and I feel terrible. I want to make it up to them. And that feeling is totally sincere – it's not an act. I'm genuinely sorry for the pain I've caused the other person."

Rage

"I wouldn't say that my rage comes from repressed self-contempt (mine is not repressed – I'm totally aware of it). And it's not missing atonement either, since I do atone. The rage comes from feeling humiliated, from feeling that the other person has somehow sadistically and gleefully made me feel inferior, that they're getting off on being superior, that they're mocking me and ridiculing me, that they have scorn and contempt for me and find it all very amusing. That – whether real or imagined (usually imagined) – is what causes my rage."

Pursuing Relationships with Narcissists

"There are some very few of us who actually seek out relationships with narcissists. We do this with the full knowledge that we are not wanted, despised even. We persist and pursue no matter the consequences, no matter the cost.

I am an 'inverted narcissist'. It is because as a child I was 'imprinted/fixated' with a particular pattern involving relationships. I was engulfed so completely by my father's personality and repressed so severely by various other factors in my childhood that I simply didn't develop a recognisable personality. I existed purely as an extension of my father. I was his genius Wunderkind. He ignored my mother and poured all his energy and effort into me. I did not develop full-blown secondary narcissism… I developed into the perfect 'other half' of the narcissists moulding me. I became the perfect, eager co-dependent. And this is an imprint, a pattern in my psyche, a way of (not) relating to the world of relationships by only being able to truly relate to one person (my father) and then one kind of person – the narcissist.

He is my perfect lover, my perfect mate, a fit that is so slick and smooth, so comfortable and effortless, so filled with meaning and actual feelings – that's the other thing. I cannot feel on my own. I am incomplete. I can only feel when I am engulfed by another (first it was my father) and now – well now it has to be a narcissist. Not just any narcissist either. He must be exceedingly smart, good looking, have adequate reproductive equipment and some knowledge on how to use it and that's about it.

When I am engulfed by someone like this I feel completed, I can actually FEEL. I am whole again. I function as a sibyl, an oracle, an extension of the narcissist. His fiercest protector, his purveyor/procurer of NS, the secretary, organiser, manager, etc. I think you get the picture and this gives me INTENSE PLEASURE.

So the answer to your question: 'Why would anyone want to be with someone who doesn't want them back?' The short answer is, 'Because there is no one else remotely worth looking at.'"

Making Amends

"I mostly apologise, and I give the person space to talk about what hurt them so that (1) they get to express their anger or hurt to me, and (2) I can understand better and know better how not to hurt them (if I can avoid it) the next time there's a conflict. Sometimes the hurt I cause is unintentional – maybe I've been insensitive or forgetful or something, in which case I feel more certain that I can avoid repeating the hurtful behaviour, since I didn't want to hurt them in the first place. If the hurt I caused has to do with my getting my trigger pulled and going into a rage, then that hurt was quite deliberate, although at the time I was unable to experience the other person as vulnerable or capable of being hurt by me. And I do realise that if that trigger is pulled again, it might happen again. But I also hope that there'll be a LITTLE TINY window where the memory of the conversation will come back to me while I'm in my rage, and I'll remember that the person really IS vulnerable. I hope that by hearing over and over that the person actually does feel hurt by what I say while in rages, that I might remember that when I am triggered and raging. So, mostly I apologise and try to communicate with the other person. I don't verbally self-flagellate, because that's manipulative. Not to say I never do that – in fact I've had a dynamic with people where I verbally put myself down and try to engage the other person into arguing me out of it.

But if I'm in the middle of apologising to the other person for hurting them, then I feel like this is their moment, and I don't want to turn the focus toward getting them to try to make me feel better. I will talk about myself, but only in an attempt to communicate, so that we can understand each other better. I might say, 'I got triggered about such-and-such, and you seemed so invulnerable that it enraged me', etc. – and the other person might react with, 'But I was feeling vulnerable, I just couldn't show it', etc. – and we'll go back and forth like that. So it's not like I don't think my feelings count, and I do want the other person to UNDERSTAND my feelings, but I don't want to put the other person in the role of taking care of my feelings in that moment, because they have just been hurt by me and I'm trying to make it up to them, not squeeze more stuff OUT of them…"

"So when I've been a real jerk to someone, I want them to feel like it's OK to be pissed off at me, and I want them to know that I am interested in and focused on how they feel, not just on how I feel. As for gifts – I used to do that, but eventually I came to feel that that was manipulative, too, that it muddled things because then the other person would feel like they couldn't be angry anymore, since after all, I've just brought them this nice gift. I also feel that in general, gift-giving is a sweet and tender thing to do, and I don't want to sully that tenderness by associating it with the hurt that comes from abusive behaviour."

Why Narcissists?

"I am BUILT this way. I may have overstated it by saying that I have 'no choice' because, in fact I do.

The choice is – live in an emotionally deadened monochrome world where I can reasonably interact with normal people OR I can choose to be with a narcissist in which case my world is Technicolor, emotionally satisfying, alive and wondrous (also can be turbulent and a real roller coaster ride for the unprepared, not to mention incredibly damaging for people who are not inverted narcissists and who fall into relationships with narcissists). As I have walked on both sides of the street, and because I have developed coping mechanisms that protect me really quite well, I can reasonably safely engage in a primary, intimate relationship with a narcissist without getting hurt by it.

The real WHY of it all is that I learned, as a young child, that being 'eaten alive' by a narcissist parent, to the point where your existence is but an extension of his own, was how all relationships ought to work. It is a psychological imprint – my 'love map', it is what feels right to me intrinsically. A pattern of living – I don't know how else to describe it so you and others will understand how very natural and normal this is for me. It is not the torturous existence that most of the survivors of narcissism are recounting on this list.

My experiences with narcissists, to me, ARE NORMAL for me. Comfortable like an old pair of slippers that fit perfectly. I don't expect many people to attempt to do this, to 'make themselves into' this kind of person. I don't think anyone could, if they tried.

It is my need to be engulfed and merged that drives me to these relationships and when I get those needs met I feel more normal, better about myself. I am the outer extension of the narcissist. In many ways I am a vanguard, a public two-way warning system, fiercely defending my narcissist from harm, and fiercely loyal to him, catering to his every need in order to protect his fragile existence. These are the dynamics of my particular version of engulfment. I don't need anyone to take care of me. I need only to be needed in this very particular way, by a narcissist who inevitably possesses the ability to engulf in a way that normal, fully realised adults cannot. It is somewhat paradoxical – I feel freer and more independent with a narcissist than without one. I achieve more in my life when I am in this form of relationship. I try harder, work harder, am more creative, think better of myself, excel in most every aspect of my life."

"…I go ahead and cater to him and pretend that his words don't hurt, and later, I engage in an internal fight with myself for being so damned submissive. It's a constant battle and I can't seem to decide which voice in my head I should listen to… I feel like a fool, yet, I would rather be a fool with him than a lonely, well-rounded woman without him. I've often said that the only way that we can stay together is because we feed off of each other. I give him everything he needs and he takes it. Seeing him happy and pleased is what gives me pleasure. I feel very successful then."

Partial NPD

"I do think it's uncommon for girls to develop these patterns, as they are usually trained to be self-effacing. I certainly was! However, I have a lot of the very same underlying patterns that full-blown, obnoxiously egotistical NP's have, but I am not egotistical because I didn't develop the pattern of inflated Ego and grandiosity. All the rest of it is there, though: fragile Ego, lack of a centre or self, super-sensitive to criticism and rejections, pathological, obsessive envy, comparisons and competitive attitudes toward others, a belief that everyone in the world is either superior or inferior to me, and so on.

Sometimes I kind of wish I had developed the inflated Ego of a complete NP, because then I would at least be able to hide from all the pain I feel. But at the same time, I'm glad I didn't, because those people have a much lower chance of recovery – how can they recover if they don't acknowledge anything is wrong? Whereas it's pretty clear to me I have problems, and I've spent my life working on them and trying to change myself and heal."

Narcissist-Non Narcissist and Narcissist-Inverted Narcissist Couples

"Can a N and a non-N ever maintain a long lasting marriage? It would seem that a non-N would have too much self-esteem to lend himself to a lifetime of catering and pandering to an N's unending need for unearned adoration and glory. I, as a non-N… got tired of these people and their unremitting attempts to drain my psyche within a relatively short period of time and abandoned them as soon as I realised what I was dealing with to preserve my own sanity."

"It depends on the non-narcissist, really. Narcissism is a RIGID, systemic pattern of responses. It is so all-pervasive and all-encompassing that it is a PERSONALITY disorder. If the non-narcissist is codependent, for instance, then the narcissist is a perfect match for him and the union will last…"

"You have to pimp for the narcissist, intellectually, and sexually. If your narcissist is somatic, you are much better off lining up the sex partners than leaving it to him. Intellectual pimping is more varied. You can think of wonderful things and then subtly string out the idea, in the most delicate of packages and watch the narcissist cogitate their way to 'their' brilliant discovery whilst you bask in the glow of their perfection and success… The point of this entire exercise is to assure YOUR supply, which is the narcissist himself, not to punish yourself by giving away a great idea or abase yourself because, of course, YOU are not worthy of having such a great idea on your own – but who knows, it may seem that way to the inverted narcissist. It really depends on how self-aware the inverted is."

"The only rejection you need to fear is the possibility of losing the narcissist and if one is doing everything else right, this is very unlikely to happen! So by 'emotionally independent' I am talking about being self-assured, doing your own thing, having a life, feeling strong and good about yourself, getting emotional sustenance from other people. I mean, let's face it, a drug is a drug is a habit. Habits just are, and what they ARE NOT are the be all and end all of love, commitment and serene symmetrical, balanced emotional perfection that is the ideal of the romanticised 'love-for-a-lifetime' all-American relationship dream."

"(I am) terribly turned on by narcissists. The most exciting moments of my life in every venue have been with narcissists. It is as if living and loving with normal people is a grey thing by comparison, not fuelled by sufficient adrenaline. I feel like a junkie, now, that I no longer permit myself the giddy pleasure of the RUSH I used to know when I was deeply and hopelessly involved with an N. I am like a lotus-eater. And I always felt guilty about this and also sorry that I ever succumbed that first time to my first narcissist lover."

"I am exactly this way and I feel exactly as you do, that the world is a sepia motion picture but when I am intimately involved with a narcissist, it breaks out into three-dimensional Technicolor and I can see and feel in ways that are not available to me otherwise. In my case I developed this (inverted narcissism) as a result of being the favourite of my father who so completely absorbed me into his personality that I was not able to develop a sense of separation. So I am stuck in this personality matrix of needing to be engulfed, adored by and completely taken over by a narcissist in my life. In turn, I worship, defend, regulate and procure Narcissistic Supply for my narcissist. It is like the mould and the moulded."

"In my case, I realise that while I can't stop loving my current narcissist, it isn't necessary for me to avoid as long as I can understand. In my way of looking at it, he is deserving of love, and since I can give him love without it hurting me, then as long as he needs it, he shall have it."

"My personal theory is that dogmatic religious culture is a retarding influence on the growth and maturation of those heavily involved – more and more autonomy (and hence personal responsibility) seems to be blithely sacrificed to the group mind/spirit. It is as though the church members become one personality and that personality is narcissistic and the individual just folds under the weight of that kind of group pressure – particularly if you are a child."

"If I displayed behaviour that made my XXX look good to others, I was insipidly overvalued. When I dared be something other than who she wanted me to be, the sarcastic criticism and total devaluation was unbelievable. So, I learned to be all things to all people. I get a heavenly high from surrendering my power to a narcissist, to catering to them, in having them overvalue and need me, and it is the only time that I truly feel alive…"

"We have very little choice in all of this. We are as vacant and warped as the narcissist. XXX is wont to say, 'I don't HAVE a personality disorder, I AM a personality disorder.' It defines who we are and how we will respond. You will always and ONLY have real feelings when you are with a narcissist. It is your love map, it is the programming within your psyche. Does it need to control your behaviour? Not necessarily. Knowing what you are can at least give you the opportunity to forecast the effect of an action before you take it. So, loveless black and white may be the very healthiest thing for you for the foreseeable future. I tend to think of these episodes with narcissists as being cyclic. You will likely need to cut loose for a while when your child is older.

DO NOT feel ashamed please! Should a physically handicapped person feel ashamed of their handicap? No and neither should we. The trouble with us is that we are fooled into thinking that these relationships are 'guilty pleasures'. They feel so very good for a time but they are more akin to addiction satisfaction rather than being the 'right match' or an 'appropriate relationship'. I am still very conflicted myself about this. I wrote a few months ago that it was like having a caged very dangerous animal inside of me. When I get near narcissists, the animal smells its own kind and it wants out. I very carefully 'micro-manage' my life. This means that I daily do fairly regular reality checks and keep a very tight reign on my self and my behaviours. I am also obsessive-compulsive."

"I feel as though I'm constantly on an emotional roller coaster. I may wake up in a good mood, but if my N partner does or says something, which is hurtful to me, my mood changes immediately. I now feel sad, empty, afraid. All I want to do at this point is anything that will make him say something NICE to me.

Once he does, I'm back on top of the world. This pattern of mood changes, or whatever you may call them, can take place several times a day. Each and every day. I've gotten to the point where I'm not sure that I can trust myself to feel any one way, because I know that I have no control over myself. He has the control. It's scary, yet I've sort of come to depend on him determining how I am going to feel."

"When I was first involved with my cerebral narcissist I was like this but after awhile I just learned to become more emotionally distant (the ups and downs were just too much) and find emotional gratification with other people, mostly girl friends and one of two male friends. I make a point of saying … that the invert must be or become emotionally and financially independent (if you don't do this he will eat you up and when he has finished with you and you are nothing but a husk, you will be expelled from his life in one big vomit). It is really important for you to start to take responsibility for your own emotional wellness without regard to how he treats you. Remember that the narcissist has the emotional maturity of a two-year old! Don't expect much in the way of emotional depth or support in your relationship – he simply is not capable of anything that sophisticated."

Return

Codependence and Dependent Personality Disorder

There is great confusion regarding the terms co-dependent, counter-dependent, and dependent. Before we proceed to study Dependent Personality Disorder in our next article, we would do well to clarify these terms.

Codependents

Like dependents (people with Dependent Personality Disorder), codependents depend on other people for their emotional gratification and the performance of both inconsequential and crucial daily and psychological functions.

Codependents are needy, demanding, and submissive. They suffer from abandonment anxiety and, to avoid being overwhelmed by it, they cling to others and act immaturely. These behaviours are intended to elicit protective responses and to safeguard the "relationship" with their companion or mate upon whom they depend. Codependents appear to be impervious to abuse. No matter how badly mistreated, they remain committed.

This is where the "co" in "co-dependence" comes into play. By accepting the role of victims, codependents seek to control their abusers and manipulate them. It is a danse macabre in which both members of the dyad collaborate.

The codependent sometimes claims to pity her abuser and cast herself in the grandiose roles of his saviour and redeemer. Her overwhelming empathy imprisons the codependent in these dysfunctional relationships and she feels guilt either because she believes that she had driven the abuser to maltreat her or because she contemplates abandoning him.

Typology of Codependents

Codependence is a complex, multi-faceted, and multi-dimensional defence against the codependent's fears and needs. There are four categories of codependence, stemming from their respective aetiologies:

(i) Codependence that aims to fend of anxieties related to abandonment. These codependents are clingy, smothering, and prone to panic, are plagued with ideas of reference, and display self-negating submissiveness. Their main concern is to prevent their victims (friends, spouses, family members) from deserting them or from attaining true autonomy and independence. These codependents merge with their "loved" ones and experience any sign of abandonment (actual, threatened, or even imagined) as a form of self-annihilation or "amputation".

(ii) Codependence that is geared to cope with the codependent's fear of losing control. By feigning helplessness and neediness such codependents coerce their environment into ceaselessly catering to their needs, wishes, and requirements. These codependents are "drama queens" and their life is a kaleidoscope of instability and chaos. They refuse to grow up and force their nearest and dearest to treat them as emotional and/or physical invalids. They deploy their self-imputed deficiencies and disabilities as weapons.

Both these types of codependents use emotional blackmail and, when necessary, threats to secure the presence and blind compliance of their "suppliers".

(iii) Vicarious codependents live through others. They "sacrifice" themselves in order to glory in the accomplishments of their chosen targets. They subsist on reflected light, on second-hand applause, and on derivative achievements. They have no personal history, having suspended their wishes, preferences, and dreams in favour of another's.

From my book "Malignant Self Love - Narcissism Revisited":

"Inverted Narcissist

Also called "covert narcissist", this is a co-dependent who depends exclusively on narcissists (narcissist-co-dependent). If you are living with a narcissist, have a relationship with one, if you are married to one, if you are working with a narcissist, etc. – it does NOT mean that you are an inverted narcissist.

To "qualify" as an inverted narcissist, you must CRAVE to be in a relationship with a narcissist, regardless of any abuse inflicted on you by him/her. You must ACTIVELY seek relationships with narcissists and ONLY with narcissists, no matter what your (bitter and traumatic) past experience has been. You must feel EMPTY and UNHAPPY in relationships with ANY OTHER kind of person. Only then, and if you satisfy the other diagnostic criteria of a Dependent Personality Disorder, can you be safely labelled an 'inverted narcissist'."

(iv) **"Codependent or Borderline narcissists"** oscillate between periods of clinging and other codependent behavior patterns (which they interpret as "intimacy") and eras of aloofness, detachment, and emotional neglect and abandonment (which they regard as legitimate and the only possible manifestations of their personal autonomy and space.) They also tend to form with their intimate partner a shared psychosis. These are all the outcomes of their overwhelming and all-pervasive abandonment anxiety: they either smother their partner in an attempt to forestall desertion – or they pre-emptively abandon ship, thus avoiding hurt and maintaining an illusion of control over the situation ("I walked out on her and dumped her, not the other way around.")

The codependent deploys strategies such as merger (becoming one with her intimate partner while renouncing all personal autonomy and independence of both of them, up to a point of shared psychosis); coextensivity (the "ventriloquist defense": insisting that the partner mind-reads her and acts in ways that reflect her inner psychological states and moods); and shifting boundaries (using behavioural unpredictability and ambient uncertainty to induce paralysing dependence in the partner.)

(v) Finally, there is another form of dependence that is so subtle that it eluded detection until very recently.

Counterdependents

Counterdependents reject and despise authority and often clash with authority figures (parents, boss, the Law). Their sense of self-worth and their very self-identity are premised on and derived from (in other words, are dependent on) these acts of bravura and defiance. They are "personal autonomy militants". Counterdependents are fiercely, militantly independent; controlling; self-centered; and aggressive. Many of them are antisocial and use Projective Identification (i.e. force people to behave in ways that buttresses and affirm the counterdependent's view of the world and his expectations).

These behavior patterns are often the result of a deep-seated fear of intimacy. In an intimate relationship, the counterdependent feels enslaved, ensnared, and captive. Counterdependents are locked into "approach-avoidance repetition complex" cycles. Hesitant approach is followed by avoidance of commitment. They are "lone wolves" and bad team players.

From my book "Malignant Self Love - Narcissism Revisited":

"Counterdependence is a reaction formation. The counterdependent dreads his own weaknesses. He seeks to overcome them by projecting an image of omnipotence, omniscience, success, self-sufficiency, and superiority.

Most "classical" (overt) narcissists are counterdependent. Their emotions and needs are buried under "scar tissue" which had formed, coalesced, and hardened during years of one form of abuse or another. Grandiosity, a sense of entitlement, a lack of empathy, and overweening haughtiness usually hide gnawing insecurity and a fluctuating sense of self-worth."

Situational Codependence

Click HERE to Watch the Video

Some patients develop codependent behaviors and traits in the wake of a life crisis, especially if it involves an abandonment and resulting solitude (e.g. divorce, or an empty nest: when one's children embark on their own, autonomous lives, or leave home altogether.)

Such late-onset codependence fosters a complex emotional and behavioral chain reaction whose role is to resolve the inner conflict by ridding oneself of the emergent, undesirable codependent conduct.

Consciously, such a patient may, at first, feel liberated. But, unconsciously, being abruptly "dumped" and lonesome has a disorienting and disconcerting effect (akin to intoxication). Many patients rush headlong and indiscriminately into new relationships. Deep inside, this kind of patient has always dreaded being lonely (lonely, not alone!). Following a divorce, the death of a significant other or intimate partner, the passing away of parents or other loved ones, children relocating to college, and similar episodes of dislocation, she suppresses this dread because she possesses no real, effective solutions and antidotes to her sudden solitude and has developed no meaningful ways to cope with it.

We are taught that denied and repressed emotions often re-emerge in camouflage, as it were. The dread of ending up all alone is such that the patient becomes codependent in order to make sure that she never finds herself in a similar situation. Her codependence is a series of dysfunctional behaviors that are intended to fend off abandonment.

Still, patients who develop situational codependence (unlike classic, lifelong codependents) are fundamentally balanced and strong personalities who cherish their self-control. So, they always keep all their options open, including the vital option of going it alone yet again. They make sure to choose the wrong partner and then they spectacularly "expose" his egregious misconduct so that they can get rid of him and of the newly-acquired codependence in good conscience and at the same time.

To reiterate:

- The situational codependent is characterized by a deep-set fear of being lonely (abandonment anxiety, a form of attachment disorder) as an underlying, dormant inner landscape;

- This lurking abandonment anxiety is awakened by life's tribulations: divorce, an empty nest, death of one's nearest and dearest.

- At first, the newly-found freedom is exhilarating and intoxicating. But this "feel-good" factor actually serves to enhance the anxiety! The inner dialog goes something like this: "What if it feels so good that I will opt to remain by myself for the rest of my days? This prospect is terrifying!"

- Thus, a conflict erupts between conscious emotions and behaviors (liberation, joy, pleasure-seeking, etc.) and a nagging unconscious anxiety ("I am not getting any younger", "This can't go on for ever", "I've got to settle down, to find an appropriate mate, not to be left alone", etc.)

- To allay this internal tension, the patient comes up with situational codependence as a coping strategy: to attract and bond with a mate, so as to forestall abandonment.

- Yet, the situational codependent is ego-dystonic. She is very unhappy with her codependence (though, at this stage, she is utterly unaware of all these dynamics.) It runs contrary to her primary nature as accomplished, assertive, self-confident person with a well-regulated sense of self-worth. She feels the need to frustrate this new set of compulsive addictions (codependence) and to get rid of it because it threatens who she is and who she thinks she is (her self-perception.) Surely, she is not the clinging, maudlin, weak, out of control type! All her life, she has known herself to be a strong, good judge of character, intelligent, and in control. Codependence doesn't become her!

But how could she get rid of it? In three easy steps:

- She chooses the wrong partner (unconsciously);

- She proves to her satisfaction that he is the wrong partner for her;

- She gets rid of him, thus re-establishing her autonomy, resilience, self-control and demonstrating credibly that she is codependent no more!

Dependent Personality Disorder is a much disputed mental health diagnosis.

We are all dependent to some degree. We all like to be taken care of. When is this need judged to be pathological, compulsive, pervasive, and excessive? Clinicians who contributed to the study of this disorder use words such as "craving", "clinging", "stifling" (both the dependent and her partner), and "humiliating", or "submissive". But these are all subjective terms, open to disagreement and differences of opinion.

Moreover, virtually all cultures encourage dependency to varying degrees. Even in developed countries, many women, the very old, the very young, the sick, the criminal, and the mentally-handicapped are denied personal autonomy and are legally and economically dependent on others (or on the authorities). Thus, the Dependent Personality Disorder is diagnosed only when such behavior does not conform to social or cultural norms.

Codependents, as they are sometimes known, are possessed with fantastic worries and concerns and are paralyzed by their abandonment anxiety and fear of separation. This inner turmoil renders them indecisive. Even the simplest everyday decision becomes an excruciating ordeal. This is why codependents rarely initiate projects or do things on their own.

Dependents typically go around eliciting constant and repeated reassurances and advice from myriad sources. This recurrent solicitation of succour is proof that the codependent seeks to transfer responsibility for his or her life to others, whether they have agreed to assume it or not.

This recoil and studious avoidance of challenges may give the wrong impression that the Dependent is indolent or insipid. Yet, most Dependents are neither. They are often fired by repressed ambition, energy, and imagination. It is their lack self-confidence that holds them back. They don't trust their own abilities and judgment.

Absent an inner compass and a realistic assessment of their positive qualities on the one hand and limitations on the other hand, Dependents are forced to rely on crucial input from the outside. Realizing this, their behavior becomes self-negating: they never disagree with meaningful others or criticizes them. They are afraid to lose their support and emotional nurturance.

Consequently, as I have written in the Open Site Encyclopedia entry on this disorder:

"The codependent moulds himself/herself and bends over backward to cater to the needs of his nearest and dearest and satisfy their every whim, wish, expectation, and demand. Nothing is too unpleasant or unacceptable if it serves to secure the uninterrupted presence of the codependent's family and friends and the emotional sustenance s/he can extract (or extort) from them.

The codependent does not feel fully alive when alone. S/he feels helpless, threatened, ill-at-ease, and child-like. This acute discomfort drives the codependent to hop from one relationship to another. The sources of nurturance are interchangeable. To the codependent, being with someone, with anyone, no matter who, is always preferable to solitude."

Read Notes from the therapy of a Dependent (Codependent) Patient

The Codependent's Inner Mother and Child

Parents of codependents teach their offspring to expect only conditional, transactional love: the child is supposed to render a service or fulfil the parent's wishes in return for affection and compassion, attention and emotion. Ineluctably, the hurt child reacts with rage to this unjust mistreatment.

With no recourse to the offending parent, this fury is either directed outwardly, at others (who stand in for the bad parent) - or inwardly. The former solution yields a psychopath, or a passive-aggressive (negativistic) - the latter solution, a masochist. Similarly, with an unavailable parent, the child's reserve of love can be directed inward, at himself (to yield a narcissist), or outward, towards others (and, thus, form a codependent.)

All these choices retard personal growth and are self-annihilating. In all four paths the adult plays the dual roles of a punitive parent and an eternal child, who is unable and unwilling to grow up for fear of incurring the wrath of the parent with whom he had merged so thoroughly early on.

When the codependent merges with a love object, she interprets her newfound attachment and bond as a betrayal of the punitive parent. She fully anticipates the internalized parent's disapproval and dreads its (self-)destructive disciplinarian measures. In an attempt to placate this implacable divinity she turns on her partner and lashes out at him, thus establishing where her true loyalties and affiliation lie (i.e., with the parent.) Concurrently, she punishes herself as she tries to pre-empt the merciless onslaught of her sadistic parental introjects and superego: she engages in a panoply of self-destructive and self-defeating behaviours.

Acutely aware of the risk of losing her partner owing to her abusive misconduct, the codependent experiences extreme abandonment anxiety. She swings wildly between self-effacing and clinging ("doormat") behaviours on the one hand and explosive, vituperative invective on the other hand: the former being the manifestations of her "eternal child" and the latter expressions of her "punitive parent".

Such abrupt shifts in affect and conduct are often misdiagnosed as the hallmarks of a mood disorder, especially Bipolar Disorder. But where Dependent Personality Disorder is diagnosed, these pendular tectonic upheavals are indicative of an underlying personality structure rather than of any biochemically-induced perturbations.

"I Can't Live Without Him/Her"

Click HERE to watch the video

Akin to addiction, dependence on other people fulfils important mental health functions. First, it is an organizing principle: it serves to explain behaviours and events within a coherent "narrative" (fictional story) or frame of reference ("I acted this way because ..."). Second, it gives meaning to life. Third: the constant ups and downs satisfy your need for excitement and thrills. Fourth, and most crucially, your addiction and emotional lability place you at the center of attention and allow you to manipulate people around you to do your bidding.

Indeed, you are convinced that you cannot live without your dependence.

This is a subtle and important distinction: you can survive without him or her, but you believe profoundly (erroneously as it happens) that you cannot go on living without your addiction to your partner. You experience your dependence as your best friend, your comfort zone, as familiar and warm and fitting as an old pair of slippers. You are addicted to and dependent on your dependence, but you attribute its source to boyfriends, mates, spouses, children, parents - anyone who happens to fit the bill and the plot of your narrative. They come and go - your addiction remains intact; they are interchangeable - your dependence is immutable.

So, what can you do about it?

Extreme cases of codependence (such as Dependent or Borderline Personality Disorders) require professional help. Luckily, dependence is a spectrum and most people with dependent traits and behaviours are clustered somewhere in the middle. Help yourself by realizing that the world never comes to end when relationships do: it is your dependence which reacts with desperation, not you. Next, analyze your addiction: what are the stories and narratives that underlie it? Do you tend to idealize your intimate partner? If so, can you see him or her in a more realistic light? Are you anxious about being abandoned? Why? Have you been traumatically abandoned in the past, as a child, perhaps? Write down the worst possible scenario: the relationship is over and s/he leaves you. Is your physical survival at stake? Of course not. Make a list of the consequences of the breakup and write, next to each one what you can and intend to do about it. Armed with this plan of action, you are bound to feel safer and more confident.

Finally, make sure to share your thoughts, fears, and emotions with friends and family. Social support is indispensable. One good friend is worth a hundred therapy sessions.

Countering Abandonment and Separation Anxiety

Click HERE to Watch the Video

Clinging and smothering behaviours are the unsavoury consequences of a deep-set existential, almost mortal fear of abandonment and separation. For the codependent to maintain a long-term, healthy relationship, she must first confront her anxieties head on. This can be done via psychotherapy: the therapeutic alliance is a contract between patient and therapist which provides for a safe environment, where abandonment is not an option and, thus, where the client can resume personal growth and form a modicum of self-autonomy. In extremis, a psychiatrist may wish to prescribe anti-anxiety medication.

Self-help is also an option, though; meditation, yoga, and the elimination of any and all addictions, such as workaholism, or binge eating. Feelings of emptiness and loneliness – at the core of abandonment anxiety and other dysfunctional attachment styles – can be countered with meaningful activities (mainly altruistic and charitable) and true, stable friends, who provide a safe haven and are unlikely to abandon her and, therefore, constitute a holding, supportive, and nourishing environment.

The codependent's reflexive responses to her inner turmoil are self-defeating and counterproductive. They often bring about the very outcomes she fears most. But these outcomes also tend to buttress her worldview ("the world is hostile, I am bound to get hurt") and sustain her comfort zone ("abuse and abandonment are familiar to me; at least I know the ropes and how to cope with them.")

This is why she needs to exit this realm of mirrored fears and fearsome mental tumult. She should adopt new avocations and hobbies, meet new people, engage is non-committal, dispensable relationships, and, in general, take life more lightly.

Some codependents develop a type of "militant independence" as a defense against their own sorely felt vulnerability (their dependence.) But even these daring "rebels" tend to view their relationships in terms of "black and white" (an infantile psychological defense mechanism known as "splitting".) They tend to regard their relationships as either doomed to failure or everlasting and their mates as both unique and indispensable ("soulmate", "twin") or completely interchangeable (objectified.)

These, of course, are misperceptions; cognitive deficits grounded in emotional immaturity and thwarted personal development. All relationships have a life expectancy, a "sell by", "good before", or expiry date. No one is irreplaceable or completely interchangeable. The codependent's problems are rooted in a profound lack of self-love and an absence of object constancy (she regards herself as unloved and unlovable when she is all by herself.)

Yet, clinging, codependent, and counterdependent (fiercely independent, defiant, and intimacy-retarding) behaviours can be modified. If you fear abandonment to the point of a phobia, here's my advice:

Compile a written, very detailed "mission statement" regarding all the aspects of your romantic relationships: how would you like them to look like and how would you go about securing the best outcomes. Revisit and revise this "charter" regularly.

List your 3 most important mate choice criteria: what would you be looking for in a first date and without which there will be no second date. This list is your filter, your proverbial selective membrane. Revisit and revise it regularly as your taste and preferences change.

Conduct a thorough background check on your prospective intimate partner. Go online and Google his name; visit his social networking accounts; ask friends and family for information and an appraisal of his character, temperament, and personality. This preparatory research will put you in control and empower you. It will serve as an antidote to uncertainty and the anxiety attendant upon it.

Next use the "Volatility Threshold" and the "Threat Monitoring" tools.

The "Volatility Threshold" instrument is a compilation of 1-3 types of behaviours that you consider critically desirable ("deal-makers") in your partner. Observe him and add up the number of times he had acted inconsistently and, thus, reversed these crucial aspects of his behavior substantially and essentially. Decide in advance how many "strikes" would constitute a "deal-breaker" and when he reaches this number – simply leave. Do not share with him either the existence or the content of this "test" lest it might affect his performance and cause him to playact and prevaricate.

As a codependent, you tend to jump to conclusions and then "jump the gun": you greatly exaggerate the significance of even minor infractions and disagreements and you are always unduly fatalistic and pessimistic about the survival chances of your relationships. The "Threat Monitoring" tool is comprised of an inventory of warning signs and red flags that, in your view and from your experience, herald and portend abandonment. The aim is to falsify this list: to prove to you that, more often than not, you are wrong in predicting a breakup.

In general, try to act as though you were a scientist: construct alternative hypotheses (interpretations of behaviours and events) to account for what you regard as transgressions and bad omens. Test these hypotheses before you decide to end it all with a grand gesture, a dramatic exit, or a decisive finale. Preemptive abandonment is based more on your insecurities than on facts, so make sure to test your hypotheses – and your partner - in a variety of settings before you call it a day and before you prophesy doom and gloom.

This "scientific" approach to your intimate relationship has the added benefit of delaying the instant alleviation of your anxiety which consists of impulsive, ill-thought actions. It takes time to form hypotheses and test them. This lapse between trigger and reaction is all you need. By the time you have formed your informed opinion, your anxiety will have abated and you will no longer feel the urge to "do something now, whatever it may be!"

Armed with these "weapons" you should feel a lot more confident as you enter a new romantic liaison. But, the secret of the longevity of long-term relationships lies in being who you are, in acting transparently, in externalizing your internal dialog and inner voices. In short: if you want your relationships to last, you should express your emotions and concerns on a regular basis. You should knowingly and willingly assume all the risks associated with doing so: of exposing the chinks in your armour; of your vulnerabilities and blind spots being abused, exploited, and leveraged; of being misunderstood, even mocked. But the rewards of being open with your partner (without being naive or gullible) are enormous and multifarious: stronger bonding often results in long-lasting relationships.

Early on you should confer with your intimate partner and inform him of what, to you, constitutes a threat: what types of conduct he should avoid and what modes of communication he should eschew. You should both agree on protocols of communication: fears, needs, triggers, wishes, boundaries, requests, priorities, and preferences should all be shared on a regular basis and in a structured and predictable manner. Remember: structure, predictability, even formality are great antidotes to anxiety.

But there is only that much that your partner can do to ameliorate your mental anguish. You can and should help him in this oft-Herculean task. You can start by using drama to desensitize yourself to your phobia. In your mind imagine and rehearse, in excruciating detail, both the worst-case and best-case scenarios (abandonment in the wake of adultery versus blissful marriage, for instance.)

In these reveries, do not act as an observer: place yourself firmly at the scene of the action and prepare detailed responses within these impromptu plays. At first, this pseudo-theatre may prove agonizing, but the more you exercise your capacity for daydreaming the more you will find yourself immune to abandonment. You may even end up laughing out loud during the more egregious scenes!

Similarly, prepare highly-detailed contingency plans of action for every eventuality, including the various ways in which your relationship can disintegrate. Be prepared for anything and everything, thoroughly and well in advance. Planning equals control and control means lessened dread.

Issues and Goals in the Treatment of Dependent Personality Disorder (Codependence, or Codependency)

ISSUE 1

The patient has alloplastic defenses and an external locus of control. Though she believes that she is in full control of her life, her behavior is mostly reactive and she is buffeted by circumstances and decisions made by other people - hence her tendency to blame the outside world for every misfortune, mishap, and defeat she endures. She rarely takes responsibility for her choices and actions and is frequently surprised and resentful when faced with the consequences of her misconduct.

The patient is convinced that she is worthless and bad, a loser and no-good. She is masochistically self-destructive and self-defeating in her romantic relationships. These propensities are compounded by a predilection to decompensate and act out, sometimes violently, when her defences fail her.

GOAL 1

To develop autoplastic defences and an internal locus of control: to learn to assume responsibility for her actions and refrain from self-destructive and self-defeating behaviors.

ISSUE 2

Having been deprived of it in her childhood, the patient is on a perpetual quest for ideal love: motherly, protective, engulfing, omnipresent, and responsive. Her mate should be handsome, sexy, and should draw attention from and elicit envy. He should be fun to be with and intelligent, although passive, malleable, compliant, and subservient.

Yet, the typical codependent has been exposed only to transactional and conditional love from her parents: love was granted in return for meeting their unrealistic and, therefore, inevitably frustrating expectations.

Such patients resort to fantasy and develop a deficient reality test when it comes to their romantic liaisons. The patient lacks self-awareness and sets conflicting goals for her intimate partners: they are supposed to provide sex, intimacy, companionship and friendship - but also agree to be objectified and to self-deny in order to fulfil their roles in the codependent's "film".

GOAL 2

To develop realistic expectations regarding love, romance, and relationships as well as relationship skills.

ISSUE 3

The narcissistic codependent idealizes her intimate romantic partners and then devalues them. She seeks to "mold" and "sculpt" them to conform to her vision of the relationship. She deprives them of their self-autonomy and makes all decisions for them. In other words: she treats them as objects, she objectifies them. Such a patient is also a verbal and, at times, physical abuser. This impoverishes her relationships and hinders the development of real intimacy and love: there is no real sharing, no discourse, common interests, or joint personal growth.

Owing to the patient's insecure attachment style and abandonment/separation anxiety, she tends to cling to her partner, monopolize his time, smother him, and secure his presence and affection with material gifts (she is a compulsive giver.) As she holds himself worthless and a loser, she finds it hard to believe that any man would attach to her voluntarily, without being bribed or coerced to do so. She tends to suspect her partner's motives and is somewhat paranoid. She is possessive and romantically jealous, though not exceedingly so. This environment tends to foster aversions in her romantic partners.

GOAL 3

To develop a productive and healthy attachment style and learn relationship skills.

ISSUE 4

The codependent's proclaimed desire for stability, safety, predictability, and reliability conflicts with her lifestyle which is itinerant, labile, chaotic, and involves addictive and reckless behaviors. Her need for drama, excitement, and thrill (adrenaline junkie) extends to her romantic relationships. Owing to her low threshold for boredom and multiple depressive, dysphoric, anhedonic, and anergic episodes, she seeks distractions and the partner to provide them. She, therefore, shows a marked preference for men with mental health issues who are likely to lead disorganized lives and to react to her abuse dramatically and theatrically.

GOAL 4

Learn how to choose partners who would bring stability and safety into the relationship and how to interact with them constructively. Learn anger management skills.

ISSUE 5

The narcissistic codependent has strong narcissistic defences, especially when it comes to maintaining her grandiosity with the aid of narcissistic supply. She needs to feel chosen and desired (a flip coin of and antidote to her fear of rejection); be the centre of attention (vicariously, via her intimate partner); and to conform to expectations, values, of judgments or her peer group, relatives, and other role models and reference figures. See: Inverted Narcissist.

GOAL 5

To develop a more realistic assessment of herself and her romantic partners and, thus, reduce her dependence on narcissistic defences and narcissistic supply.

The Dependent Patient - A Case Study

Notes of first therapy session with Mona, female, 32, diagnosed with Dependent Personality Disorder (or Codependence)

"I know I won't actually die, but it often feels like it." - says Mona and nervously pats her auburn hair - "I can't live without him, that's for sure. When he is gone, it's like life switching from Technicolor to black and white. There is no excitement, this electricity in the air that seems to constantly surround him." She misses him so much that it physically hurts. Sometimes she feels like throwing up at the mere thought of separating or being abandoned by him. She is helpless without him: "He is so masterful and knows how to fix things around the house." He is gorgeous and a great lover.

Is he intellectually stimulating? Do they talk a lot? She moves uncomfortably in her seat: "He is more the silent strong type." She is supporting him financially. "He is studying". In the last seven years he had switched from psychology to political science to physical therapy. How long will she underwrite his quest for self-realization? "As long as it takes. I love him".

She acknowledges that he is verbally and sometimes physically abusive. He has cheated on her more times than she can count, usually with classmates at the university. So, why is she still with him? "He has his good sides". Do they outweigh his bad ones? She is evidently displeased with my question but is reluctant to express her reservations.

I tell her that - her intimate partner having refused to attend therapy - I am merely trying to get to know him better if only by proxy. Evidently something is bothering her, otherwise we wouldn't be having this therapy session. "I want to learn how to hold on to him."- she whispers - "He is a very special man and has special needs. I am looking for guidance on how to hook him. I want him to become addicted to me, like a junkie." She even participated in group sex once or twice to make his fantasies come true.

Does this strike her as the basis for a healthy relationship? She doesn't care. She consulted all her friends and even casual acquaintances but she doesn't know whether to trust them. Does she have many friends? Not any more. Why not? People get tired of her, they say that she is clinging. But that's not true - she only asks their advice on a regular basis. "What are friends for, anyhow?"

Does she have a job? She is a lawyer, but her dream is to become a film director. She vividly and enthusiastically describes what she would do behind the camera. What's holding her back? She laughs self-deprecatingly: "Except for mediocre talent, nothing."

Return

Narcissists, Inverted Narcissists and Schizoids

Narcissistic Personality Disorder and Schizoid Personality Disorder share the same aetiology, psychodynamics, traits (such as grandiosity) and behavior patterns.

Question:

Some narcissists are not gregarious. They avoid social events and are stay-at-home recluses. Doesn't this behaviour go against the grain of narcissism?

Answer:

I. The Common Psychological Constructs of Narcissistic and Schizoid Disorders

Click here to read the definition of the Schizoid Personality Disorder (SPD) in the DSM-IV-TR [2000].

Click here to read a description of the Schizoid Personality Disorder (SPD) and some treatment notes.

Or, as the Howard H. Goldman (Ed.) in the "Review of General Psychiatry" [4th Edition. London, Prentice Hall International, 1995] puts it:

"The person with Schizoid Personality Disorder sustains a fragile emotional equilibrium by avoiding intimate personal contact and thereby minimising conflict that is poorly tolerated."

Schizoids are often described, even by their nearest and dearest, in terms of automata ("robots"). They are uninterested in social relationships or interactions and have a very limited emotional repertoire. It is not that they do not have emotions, but they express them poorly and intermittently. They appear cold and stunted, flat, and "zombie"-like.

Consequently, these people are loners. They confide only in first-degree relatives, but maintain no close bonds or associations, not even with their immediate family. Naturally, they gravitate into solitary activities and find solace and safety in being constantly alone. Their sexual experiences are sporadic and limited and, finally, they cease altogether.

Schizoids are anhedonic - find nothing pleasurable and attractive - but not necessarily dysphoric (sad or depressed). Some schizoid are asexual and resemble the cerebral narcissist. They pretend to be indifferent to praise, criticism, disagreement, and corrective advice (though, deep inside, they are not). They are creatures of habit, frequently succumbing to rigid, predictable, and narrowly restricted routines.

Intuitively, a connection between SPD and Narcissistic Personality Disorder (NPD) seems plausible. After all, narcissists are people who self-sufficiently withdraw from others. They love themselves in lieu of loving others. Lacking empathy, they regard others as mere instruments, objectified "Sources" of Narcissistic Supply.

The inverted narcissist (IN) is a narcissist who "projects" his narcissism onto another narcissist. The mechanism of projective identification allows the IN to experience his own narcissism vicariously, through the agency of a classic narcissist. But the IN is no less a narcissist than the classical one. He is no less socially reclusive.

A distinction must be made between social interactions and social relationships. The schizoid, the narcissist and the inverted narcissist – all interact socially. But they fail to form human and social relationships (bonds). The schizoid is uninterested and the narcissist is both uninterested and incapable to due to his lack of empathy and pervasive sense of grandiosity.

The psychologist H. Deutsch first suggested the construct of "as-if personality" in the context of schizoid patients (in an article, published in 1942 and titled "Some forms of emotional disturbance and their relationship to schizophrenia"). A decade later, Winnicott named the very same idea as the "False-self Personality". The False Self has thus been established as the driving engine of both pathological narcissism and pathological schizoid states.

Both C. R. Cloninger and N. McWilliams (in "Psychoanalytic Diagnosis", 1994) observed the "faintly contemptuous (attitude) ... (and) isolated superiority" of the schizoid - clearly narcissistic traits.

Theodore Millon and Roger Davis summed it up in their seminal tome, "Personality Disorders in Modern Life" (2000):

"Where withdrawal has an arrogant or oppositional quality, fantasy in a schizoidlike person sometimes betrays the presence of a secret grandiose self that longs for respect and recognition while offsetting fears that the person is really an iconoclastic freak. These individuals combine aspects of the compensating narcissist with the autistic isolation of the schizoid, while lacking the asocial and anhedonic qualities of the pure prototype." (p. 328)

II. Cultural Considerations in Narcissistic and Schizoid Disorders

The ethno-psychologist George Devereux [Basic Problems of Ethno-Psychiatry, University of Chicago Press, 1980] proposed to divide the unconscious into the Id (the part that is instinctual and unconscious) and the "ethnic unconscious" (repressed material that was once conscious). The latter includes all the defence mechanisms and most of the Superego.

Culture dictates what is to be repressed. Mental illness is either idiosyncratic (cultural directives are not followed and the individual is unique, eccentric, and schizophrenic) – or conformist, abiding by the cultural dictates of what is allowed and disallowed.

Our culture, according to Christopher Lasch, teaches us to withdraw inwards when confronted with stressful situations. It is a vicious circle. One of the main stressors of modern society is alienation and a pervasive sense of isolation. The solution our culture offers – to further withdraw – only exacerbates the problem.

Richard Sennett expounded on this theme in "The Fall of Public Man: On the Social Psychology of Capitalism" [Vintage Books, 1978]. One of the chapters in Devereux's aforementioned tome is entitled "Schizophrenia: An Ethnic Psychosis, or Schizophrenia without Tears". To him, the United States is afflicted by what came later to be called a "schizoid disorder".

C. Fred Alford [in Narcissism: Socrates, the Frankfurt School and Psychoanalytic Theory, Yale University Press, 1988] enumerates the symptoms:

"...withdrawal, emotional aloofness, hyporeactivity (emotional flatness), sex without emotional involvement, segmentation and partial involvement (lack of interest and commitment to things outside oneself), fixation on oral-stage issues, regression, infantilism and depersonalisation. These, of course, are many of the same designations that Lasch employs to describe the culture of narcissism. Thus, it appears, that it is not misleading to equate narcissism with schizoid disorder." [Page 19]

III. The Common Psychodynamic Roots of Narcissistic and Schizoid Disorders

The first to seriously consider the similarity, if not outright identity, between the schizoid and the narcissistic disorders was Melanie Klein. She broke ranks with Freud in that she believed that we are born with a fragile, brittle, weak and unintegrated Ego. The most primordial human fear is the fear of disintegration (death), according to Klein.

Thus, the infant is forced to employ primitive defence mechanisms such as splitting, projection and introjection to cope with this fear (actually, with the result of aggression generated by the Ego). The Ego splits and projects this part (death, disintegration, aggression). It does the same with the life-related, constructive, integrative part of itself.

As a result of all these mechanics, the infant views the world as either "good" (satisfying, complying, responding, gratifying) – or bad (frustrating). Klein called it the good and the bad "breasts". The child then proceeds to introject (internalise and assimilate) the good object while keeping out (defending against) the bad objects. The good object becomes the nucleus of the forming Ego. The bad object is felt as fragmented. But it has not vanished, it is there.

The fact that the bad object is "out there", persecutory, threatening – gives rise to the first schizoid defence mechanisms, foremost amongst them the mechanism of "projective identification" (so often employed by narcissists). The infant projects parts of himself (his organs, his behaviours, his traits) unto the bad object. This is the famous Kleinian "paranoid-schizoid position". The Ego is split.

This is as terrifying as it sounds but it allows the baby to make a clear distinction between the "good object" (inside him) and the "bad object" (out there, split from him). If this phase is not transcended the individual develops schizophrenia and a fragmentation of the self.

Around the third or fourth month of life, the infant realises that the good and the bad objects are really facets of one and the same object. He develops the depressive position. This depression [Klein believes that the two positions continue throughout life] is a reaction of fear and anxiety.

The infant feels guilty (at his own rage) and anxious (lest his aggression harms the object and eliminates the source of good things). He experiences the loss of his own omnipotence since the object is now outside his self. The infant wishes to erase the results of his own aggression by "making the object whole again". By recognising the wholeness of other objects, the infant comes to realise and to experience his own wholeness. The Ego re-integrates.

But the transition from the paranoid-schizoid position to the depressive one is by no means smooth and assured. Excess anxiety and envy can delay it or prevent it altogether. Envy seeks to destroy all good objects, so that others don't have them. It, therefore, hinders the split between the good and the bad "breasts". Envy destroys the good object but leaves the persecutory, bad object intact.

Moreover, envy does not allow re-integration ["reparation" in Kleinian jargon] to take place. The more whole the object – the greater the destructive envy. Thus, envy feeds on its own outcomes. The more envy, the less integrated the Ego is, the weaker and more inadequate it is – and the more reason for envying the good object and other people.

Both the narcissist and the schizoid are examples of development arrested due to envy and other transformations of aggression.

Consider pathological narcissism.

Envy is the hallmark of narcissism and the prime source of what is known as narcissistic rage. The schizoid self – fragmented, weak, primitive – is intimately connected with narcissism through envy. Narcissists prefer to destroy themselves and to deny themselves rather than endure someone else's happiness, wholeness and "triumph".

The narcissist fails his exams in order to frustrate the teacher he adores and envies. He aborts his therapy in order not to give the therapist a reason to feel gratified. By self-defeating and self-destructing, narcissists deny the worth of others. If the narcissist fails in therapy – his analyst must be inept. If he destroys himself by consuming drugs – his parents are blameworthy and should feel guilty and bad. One cannot exaggerate the importance of envy as a motivating power in the narcissist's life.

The psychodynamic connection is obvious. Envy is a rage reaction to not controlling or "having" or engulfing the good, desired object. Narcissists defend themselves against this acidulous, corroding sensation by pretending that they do control, possess and engulf the good object. This are the narcissist's "grandiose fantasies (of omnipotence or omniscience)".

But, in doing so, the narcissist must deny the existence of any good outside himself. The narcissist defends himself against raging, all consuming envy – by solipsistically claiming to be the only good object in the world. This is an object that cannot be had by anyone, except the narcissist and, therefore, is immune to the narcissist's threatening, annihilating envy.

In order to refrain from being "owned" by anyone (and, thus, avoid self-destruction in the hands of his own envy), the narcissist reduces others to "non-entities" (the narcissistic solution), or completely avoids all meaningful contact with them (the schizoid solution).

The suppression of envy is at the core of the narcissist's being. If he fails to convince his self that he is the only good object in the universe, he is bound to be exposed to his own murderous envy. If there are others out there who are better than him, he envies them, he lashes out at them ferociously, uncontrollably, madly, hatefully and spitefully, he tries to eliminate them.

If someone tries to get emotionally intimate with the narcissist, she threatens the grandiose belief that no one but the narcissist can possess the good object (that is the narcissist himself).

Only the narcissist can own himself, have access to himself, possess himself. This is the only way to avoid seething envy and certain self-annihilation. Perhaps it is clearer now why narcissists react as raving madmen to anything, however minute, however remote that seems to threaten their grandiose fantasies, the only protective barrier between themselves and their lethal, seething envy.

There is nothing new in trying to link narcissism to schizophrenia. Freud did as much in his "On Narcissism" [1914]. Klein's contribution was the introduction of immediately post-natal internal objects. Schizophrenia, she proposed, was a narcissistic and intense relationship with internal objects (such as fantasies or images, including fantasies of grandeur). She proposed a new language.

Freud suggested a transition from (primary, object-less) narcissism (self-directed libido) to objects relations (objects directed libido). Klein suggested a transition from internal objects to external ones. While Freud thought that the denominator common to narcissism and schizoid phenomena is a withdrawal of libido from the world – Klein suggested it was a fixation on an early phase of relating to internal objects.

But is the difference not merely semantic?

"The term 'narcissism' tends to be employed diagnostically by those proclaiming loyalty to the drive model [Otto Kernberg and Edith Jacobson, for instance – SV] and mixed model theorists [Kohut], who are interested in preserving a tie to drive theory. 'Schizoid' tends to be employed diagnostically by adherents of relational models [Fairbairn, Guntrip], who are interested in articulating their break with drive theory... These two differing diagnoses and accompanying formulations are applied to patients who are essentially similar, by theorists who start with very different conceptual premises and ideological affiliations."

(Greenberg and Mitchell. Object Relations in Psychoanalytic Theory. Harvard University Press, 1983)

Klein, in effect, said that drives (e.g., the libido) are relational flows. A drive is the mode of relationship between an individual and his objects (internal and external). Thus, a retreat from the world [Freud] into internal objects [as postulated by object relations theorists and especially the British school of Fairbairn and Guntrip] – is the drive itself.

Drives are orientations (to external or internal objects). Narcissism is an orientation (a preference, we could say) towards internal objects – the very definition of schizoid phenomena as well. This is why narcissists feel empty, fragmented, "unreal", and diffuse. It is because their Ego is still split (never integrated) and because they had withdrawn from the world (of external objects).

Kernberg identifies these internal objects with which the narcissist maintains a special relationship with the idealised, grandiose images of the narcissist's parents. He believes that the narcissist's very Ego (self-representation) had fused with these parental images.

Fairbairn's work – even more than Kernberg's, not to mention Kohut's – integrates all these insights into a coherent framework. Guntrip elaborated on it and together they created one of the most impressive theoretical bodies in the history of psychology.

Fairbairn internalised Klein's insights that drives are object-orientated and their goal is the formation of relationships and not primarily the attainment of pleasure. Pleasurable sensations are the means to achieve relationships. The Ego does not seek to be stimulated and pleased but to find the right, "good", supporting object. The infant is fused with his Primary Object, the mother.

Life is not about using objects for pleasure under the supervision of the Ego and Superego, as Freud suggested. Life is about separating, differentiating, individuating, and achieving independence from the Primary Object and the initial state of fusion with it. Dependence on internal objects is narcissism. Freud's post-narcissistic (anaclitic) phase of life can be either dependent (immature) or mature.

The newborn's Ego is looking for objects with which to form relationships. Inevitably, some of these objects and some of these relationships frustrate the infant and disappoint him. He compensates for these setbacks by creating compensatory internal objects. The initially unitary Ego thus fragments into a growing group of internal objects. Reality breaks our hearts and minds, according to Fairbairn. The Ego and its objects are "twinned" and the Ego is split in three [or four, according to Guntrip, who introduced a fourth Ego]. A schizoid state ensues.

The "original" (Freudian or libidinal) Ego is unitary, instinctual, needy and object seeking. It then fragments as a result of the three typical interactions with the mother (gratification, disappointment and deprivation). The central Ego idealises the "good" parents. It is conformist and obedient. The antilibidinal Ego is a reaction to frustrations. It is rejecting, harsh, unsatisfying, dead set against one's natural needs. The libidinal Ego is the seat of cravings, desires and needs. It is active in that it keeps seeking objects to form relationships with. Guntrip added the regressed Ego, which is the True Self in "cold storage", the "lost heart of the personal self".

Fairbairn's definition of psychopathology is quantitative. How much of the Ego is dedicated to relationships with internal objects rather than with external ones (e.g., real people)? In other words: how fragmented (how schizoid) is the Ego?

To achieve a successful transition from focusing on internal objects to seeking external ones, the child needs to have the right parents (in Winnicott's parlance, the "good enough mother" – not perfect, but "good enough"). The child internalises the bad aspects of his parents in the form of internal, bad objects and then proceeds to suppress them, together ("twinned") with portions of his Ego.

Thus, his parents become a part of the child (though a repressed part). The more bad objects are repressed, the "less Ego is left" for healthy relationships with external objects. To Fairbairn, the source of all psychological disturbances is in these schizoid phenomena. Later developments (such as the Oedipus Complex) are less crucial.

Fairbairn and Guntrip think that if a person is too attached to his compensatory internal objects – he finds it hard to mature psychologically. Maturing is about letting go of internal objects. Some people just don't want to mature, or are reluctant to do so, or are ambivalent about it. This reluctance, this withdrawal to an internal world of representations, internal objects and broken Ego – is narcissism itself. Narcissists simply don't know how to be themselves, how to be and act independent while managing their relationships with other people.

Both Otto Kernberg and Franz Kohut contended that narcissism is somewhere between neurosis and psychosis. Kernberg thought that it was a borderline phenomenon, on the verge of psychosis (where the Ego is completely shattered). In this respect Kernberg, more than Kohut, identifies narcissism with schizoid phenomena and with schizophrenia. This is not the only difference between them.

They also disagree on the developmental locus of narcissism. Kohut thinks that narcissism is an early phase of development, fossilised, and doomed to be repeated (a repetition complex) while Kernberg maintains that the narcissistic self is pathological from its very inception.

Kohut believes that the narcissist's parents failed to provide him with assurances that he does possess a self (in his words, they failed to endow him with a self-object). They did not explicitly recognise the child's nascent self, its separate existence, and its boundaries. The child learned to have a schizoid, split, fragmented self, rather than a coherent ad integrated one. To Kohut, narcissism is really all-pervasive, at the very core of being (whether in its mature form, as self-love, or in it regressive, infantile form as a narcissistic disorder).

Kernberg regards "mature narcissism" (also espoused by neo-Freudians like Grunberger and Chasseguet-Smirgel) as a contradiction in terms, an oxymoron. He observes that narcissists are already grandiose and schizoid (detached, cold, aloof, asocial) at an early age (when they are three years old, according to him!).

Like Klein, Kernberg believes that narcissism is a last ditch effort (defence) to halt the emergence of the paranoid-schizoid position described by Klein. In an adult such an emergence is known as "psychosis" and this is why Kernberg classifies narcissists as borderline (almost) psychotics.

Even Kohut, who is an opponent of Kernberg's classification, uses Eugene O'Neill's famous sentence [in "The Great God Brown"]: "Man is born broken. He lives by mending. The grace of God is glue." Kernberg himself sees a clear connection between schizoid phenomena (such as alienation in modern society and subsequent withdrawal) and narcissistic phenomena (inability to form relationships or to make commitments or to empathise).

Fred Alford in "Narcissism: Socrates, the Frankfurt School and Psychoanalytic Theory" [Yale University Press, 1988] wrote:

"Fairbairn and Guntrip represent the purest expression of object relations theory, which is characterised by the insight that real relationships with real people build psychic structure. Although they rarely mention narcissism, they see a schizoid split in the self as characteristic of virtually all-emotional disorder. It is Greenberg and Mitchell, in Object Relations in Psychoanalytic Theory who establish the relevance of Fairbairn and Guntrip … by pointing out that what American analysts label 'narcissism', British analysts tend to call 'Schizoid Personality Disorder'. This insight allows us to connect the symptomatology of narcissism – feelings of emptiness, unreality, alienation and emotional withdrawal – with a theory that sees such symptoms as an accurate reflection of the experience of being split-off from a part of oneself. That narcissism is such a confusing category is in large part because its drive-theoretic definition, the libidinal cathexis of the self – in a word, self-love – seems far removed from the experience of narcissism, as characterised by a loss of, or split-in, the self. Fairbairn's and Guntrip's view of narcissism as an excessive attachment of the Ego to internal objects (roughly analogous to Freud's narcissistic, as

opposed to object, love), resulting in various splits in the Ego necessary to maintain these attachments, allows us to penetrate this confusion." [Page 67]

IV. The "Lone Wolf" Narcissist

Click HERE to Watch the Video

The narcissist's False Self requires constant dollops of narcissistic supply (attention.) The narcissist's sense of entitlement and innate superiority collide painfully with his unmitigated dependence on other people for the regulation of his labile sense of self-worth and the maintenance of his grandiose fantasies. Narcissists who are also psychopaths (antisocial) or schizoids choose to avoid the constant hurt and injuries entailed by this conflict by withdrawing from society – physically as well as psychologically - into a cocoon of self-delusion, confabulated narratives, and vivid dreams of triumph and revenge. They become "lone wolf" narcissists and prey on society at large by indiscriminately victimizing, abusing, and attacking any of person unfortunate enough to cross their path.

Inevitably, the lone wolf narcissist is in a constant state of deficient narcissistic supply, very much like a junkie deprived of access to his drug of choice. This overwhelming, unquenched, vampiric hunger coupled with an almost-psychotic state render the lone wolf narcissist dangerous to others. His aggression often turns to outright violence; his frustration to vindictive rage; his addiction to narcissistic supply drives him to coerce people – often randomly selected – to serve as sources of adulation, affirmation, and support; his detachment evolves into a loss of touch with reality, cognitive deficits, and utter misjudgement of his environment and milieu; he seeks fame and celebrity by all means available to him, even by resorting to crime and terrorism.

V. Rationalizing a Schizoid Existence: Solitude as a Logical Choice

Click HERE to Watch the Video

"Purebred" schizoids shrug off their disorder: they simply don't like being around people and they resent the pathologizing of their lifestyle "choice" to remain aloof and alone. They consider the diagnosis of Schizoid Personality Disorder to be spurious, a mere reflection of current social coercive mores, and a culture-bound artefact.

Narcissists, as usual, tend to rationalize and aggrandize their schizoid conduct. They propound the idea that being alone is the only logical choice in today's hostile, anomic, and atomized world. The concept of "individual" exists only in the human species. Animals flock together or operate in colonies and herds. Each member of these aggregates is an extension of the organic whole. In contradistinction, people band and socialize only for purposes of a goal-oriented cooperation or the seeking of emotional rewards (solace, succour, love, support, etc.)

Yet, in contemporary civilization, the accomplishment of most goals is outsourced to impersonal collectives such as the state or large corporations. Everything from food production and distribution to education is now relegated to faceless, anonymous entities, which require little or no social interaction. Additionally, new technologies empower the individual and render him or her self-sufficient, profoundly independent of others.

As they have grown in complexity and expectations (fed by the mass media) relationships have mutated to being emotionally unrewarding and narcissistically injurious to the point of becoming a perpetual fount of pain and unease. More formalized social interactions present a substantial financial and emotional risk. Close to half of all marriages, for instance, end in a divorce, inflicting enormous pecuniary damage and emotional deprivation on the parties involved. The prevailing ethos of gender wars as reflected in the evolving legal milieu further serves to deter any residual predilection and propensity to team up and bond.

This is a vicious circle that is difficult to break: traumatized by past encounters and liaisons, people tend to avoid future ones. Deeply wounded, they are rendered less tolerant, more hypervigilant, more defensive, and more aggressive – traits which bode ill for their capacity to initiate, sustain, and maintain relationships. The breakdown and dysfunction of societal structures and institutions, communities, and social units is masked by technologies which provide verisimilitudes and confabulations. We all gravitate towards a delusional and fantastic universe of our own making as we find the real one too hurtful to endure.

Modern life is so taxing and onerous and so depletes the individual's scarce resources that little is left to accommodate the needs of social intercourse. People's energy, funds, and wherewithal are stretched to the breaking point by the often conflicting demands of mere survival in post-industrial societies. Furthermore, the sublimation of instinctual urges to pair (libido), associate, mingle, and fraternize is both encouraged and rewarded. Substitutes exist for all social functions, including sex (porn) and childrearing (single parenthood) rendering social institutions obsolete and superfluous social give-and-take awkward and inefficient.

The individual "me" has emerged as the organizing principle in human affairs, supplanting the collective. The idolatry of the individual inexorably and ineluctably results in the malignant forms of narcissism that are so prevalent – indeed, all-pervasive – wherever we direct our gaze.

Return

Schizoid Personality Disorder

Schizoids enjoy nothing and seemingly never experience pleasure (they are anhedonic). Even their nearest and dearest often describe them as "automata", "robots", or "machines". But the schizoid is not depressed or dysphoric, merely indifferent. Schizoids are uninterested in social relationships and bored or puzzled by interpersonal interactions. They are incapable of intimacy and have a very limited range of emotions and affect. Rarely does the schizoid express feelings, either negative (anger) or positive (happiness).

Schizoids never pursue an opportunity to develop a close relationship. Schizoids are asexual - not interested in sex. Consequently, they appear cold, aloof, bland, stunted, flat, and "zombie"-like. They derive no satisfaction from belonging to a close-knit group: family, church, workplace, neighborhood, or nation. They rarely marry or have children.

Schizoids are loners. Given the option, they invariably pursue solitary activities or hobbies. Inevitably, they prefer mechanical or abstract tasks and jobs that require such skills. Many computer hackers, crackers, and programmers are schizoids, for instance - as are some mathematicians and theoretical physicists. Schizoids are inflexible in their reactions to changing life circumstances and developments - both adverse and opportune. Faced with stress they may disintegrate, decompensate, and experience brief psychotic episodes or a depressive illness.

Schizoids have few friends or confidants. They trust only first-degree relatives - but, even so, they maintain no close bonds or associations, not even with their immediate family.

Schizoids pretend to be indifferent to praise, criticism, disagreement, and corrective advice (though, deep inside, they are not). They are creatures of habit, frequently succumbing to rigid, predictable, and narrowly restricted routines. From the outside, the schizoid's life looks "rudderless" and adrift.

Like people with Asperger's Syndrome, schizoids fail to respond appropriately to social cues and rarely reciprocate gestures or facial expressions, such as smiles. As the DSM-IV-TR puts it, "they seem socially inept or superficial and self-absorbed". Some narcissists are also schizoids.

The Schizoid Patient - A Case Study

Notes of first therapy session with Mark, male, 36, diagnosed with Schizoid Personality Disorder

Mark sits where instructed, erect but listless. When I ask him how he feels about attending therapy, he shrugs and mumbles "OK, I guess". He rarely twitches or flexes his muscles or in any way deviates from the posture he has assumed early on. He reacts with invariable, almost robotic equanimity to the most intrusive queries on my part. He shows no feelings when we discuss his uneventful childhood, his parents ("of course I love them"), and sad and happy moments he recollects at my request.

Mark veers between being bored with our encounter and being annoyed by it. How would he describe his relationships with other people? He has none that he can think of. In whom does he confide? He eyes me quizzically: "confide?" Who are his friends? Does he have a girlfriend? No. He shares pressing problems with his mother and sister, he finally remembers. When was the last time he spoke to them? More than two years ago, he thinks.

He doesn't seem to feel uneasy when I probe into his sex life. He smiles: no, he is not a virgin. He has had sex once with a much older woman who lived across the hall in his apartment block. That was the only time, he found it boring. He prefers to compile computer programs and he makes nice money doing it. Is he a member of a team? He involuntarily recoils: no way! He is his own boss and likes to work alone. He needs his solitude to think and be creative.

That's precisely why he is here: his only client now insists that he collaborates with the IT department and he feels threatened by the new situation. Why? He ponders my question at length and then: "I have my working habits and my long-established routines. My productivity depends on strict adherence to these rules." Has he ever tried to work outside his self-made box? No, he hasn't and has no intention of even trying it: "If it works don't fix it and never argue with success."

If he is such a roaring success what is he doing on my proverbial couch? He acts indifferent to my barb but subtly counterattacks: "Thought I'd give it a try. Some people go to one type of witch doctor, I go to another."

Does he have any hobbies? Yes, he collects old sci-fi magazines and comics. What gives him pleasure? Work does, he is a workaholic. What about his collections? "They are distractions". But do they make him happy, does he look forward to the time he spends with them? He glowers at me, baffled: " I collect old magazines." - he explains patiently - "How are old magazines supposed to make me happy?"

Return

Avoidant Personality Disorder

People suffering from Avoidant Personality Disorder feel inadequate, unworthy, inferior, and lacking in self-confidence. As a result, they are shy and socially inhibited. Aware of their real (and, often, imagined) shortcomings, they are constantly on the lookout, are hypervigilant and hypersensitive. Even the slightest, most constructive and well-meant or helpful criticism and disagreement are perceived as complete rejection, ridicule, and shaming. Consequently, they go to great lengths to avoid situations that require interpersonal contact - such as attending school, making new friends, accepting a promotion, or teamwork activities. Hence Avoidant Personality Disorder.

Inevitably, Avoidants find it difficult to establish intimate relationships. They "test' the potential friend, mate, or spouse to see whether they accept them uncritically and unconditionally. They demand continue verbal reassurances that they really wanted, desired, loved, or cared about.

When asked to describe Avoidants, people often use terms such as shy, timid, lonely, isolated, "invisible", quiet, reticent, unfriendly, tense, risk-averse, resistant to change (reluctant), restricted, "hysterical", and inhibited.

Avoidance is a self-perpetuating vicious cycle: the Avoidant's stilted mannerisms, fears for her personal safety and security, and stifled conduct elicit the very ridicule and derision that he or she so fears!

Even when confronted with incontrovertible evidence to the contrary, Avoidants doubt that they are socially competent or personally appealing. Rather than let go of their much cherished self-image, they sometimes develop persecutory delusions. For instance, they may regard honest praise as flattery and a form of attempted manipulation. Avoidants ceaselessly fantasize about ideal relationships and how they would outshine everyone else in social interactions but are unable to do anything to realize their Walter Mitty fantasies.

In public settings, Avoidants tend to keep to themselves and are very reticent. When pressed, they self-deprecate, act overly modest, and minimize the value of their skills and contributions. By doing so, they are trying to preempt what they believe to be inevitable forthcoming criticism by colleagues, spouses, family members, and friends.

From the entry I wrote for the Open Site Encyclopedia:

The disorder affects 0.5-1% of the general population (or up to 10% of outpatients seen in mental clinics). It is often comorbid with certain Mood and Anxiety Disorders, with the Dependent and Borderline Personality Disorders, and with the Cluster A personality disorder (Paranoid, Schizoid, and Schizotypal).

The Avoidant Patient - A Case Study

Notes of first therapy session with Gladys, female, 26, diagnosed with Avoidant Personality Disorder

"I would like to be normal" - says Gladys and blushes purple. In which sense is she abnormal? She prefers reading books and watching movies with her elderly mother to going out with her colleagues to the occasional office party. Maybe she doesn't feel close to them? How long has she been working with these people? Eight years in the same firm and "not one raise in salary" - she blurts out, evidently hurt. Her boss bullies her publicly and the searing shame of it all prevents her from socializing with peers, suppliers, and clients.

Does she have a boyfriend? I must be mocking her. Who would date an ugly duckling, plain secretary like her? I disagree wholeheartedly and in details with her self-assessment. I think that she is very intelligent. She half rises from her seat then thinks better of it: "Please, doctor, there no need to lie to me just in order to make me feel better. I know my good sides and they don't amount to much. If we disagree on this crucial point, perhaps I should start looking for another therapist."

A glass of water and mounds of tissue paper later, we are back on track. She dreads the idea of group therapy. "I am a social cripple. I can't work with other people. I declined a promotion to avoid working in a team." Her boss thought highly of her until she turned his offer down, so in effect it's all her fault and she has earned the abuse she is being subjected to on a daily basis. And, anyhow, he overestimated her capabilities and skills.

Why can't she interact with her co-workers? "Well, that's precisely what we are supposed to find out, isn't it?" - she retorts. Everyone is too critical and opinionated and she can't stand it. She accepts people as they are, unconditionally - why can't they treat her the same way? She fantasizes about getting married one day to a soulmate, someone who would love and cherish her regardless of her blemishes.

I ask her to describe how she thinks she is being perceived by others. "Shy, timid, lonely, isolated, invisible, quiet, reticent, unfriendly, tense, risk-averse, resistant to change, reluctant, restricted, hysterical, and inhibited." That's quite a list, I comment, now how does she view herself? The same, she largely agrees with people's perceptions of her "but it doesn't give them the right to ridicule or torment her just because she is different."

Return

Negativistic (Passive-Aggressive) Personality Disorder

Negativistic (Passive-Aggressive) Personality Disorder is not yet recognized by the DSM Committee. It makes its appearances in Appendix B of the Diagnostic and Statistical Manual, titled "Criteria Sets and Axes Provided for Further Study."

Some people are perennial pessimists and have "negative energy" and negativistic attitudes ("good things don't last", "it doesn't pay to be good", "the future is behind me"). Not only do they disparage the efforts of others, but they make it a point to resist demands to perform in workplace and social settings and to frustrate people's expectations and requests, however reasonable and minimal they may be. Such persons regard every requirement and assigned task as impositions, reject authority, resent authority figures (boss, teacher, parent-like spouse), feel shackled and enslaved by commitment, and oppose relationships that bind them in any manner.

Whether these attitudes and behaviors are acquired/learned or the outcome of heredity is still an open question. Often, passive-aggression is the only weapon of the weak and the meek, besieged as they are by frustration, helplessness, envy and spite, the organizing principles of their emotional landscape and the engines and main motivating forces of their lives.

Passive-aggressiveness wears a multitudes of guises: procrastination, malingering, perfectionism, forgetfulness, neglect, truancy, intentional inefficiency, stubbornness, and outright sabotage. This repeated and advertent misconduct has far reaching effects. Consider the Negativist in the workplace: he or she invests time and efforts in obstructing their own chores and in undermining relationships. But, these self-destructive and self-defeating behaviors wreak havoc throughout the workshop or the office.

People diagnosed with Negativistic (Passive-Aggressive) Personality Disorder resemble narcissists in some important respects. Despite the obstructive role they play, passive-aggressives feel unappreciated, underpaid, cheated, and misunderstood. They chronically complain, whine, carp, and criticize. They blame their failures and defeats on others, posing as martyrs and victims of a corrupt, inefficient, and heartless system (in other words, they have alloplastic defenses and an external locus of control).

Passive-aggressives sulk and give the "silent treatment" in reaction to real or imagined slights. They suffer from ideas of reference (believe that they are the butt of derision, contempt, and condemnation) and are mildly paranoid (the world is out to get them, which explains their personal misfortune). In the words of the DSM: "They may be sullen, irritable, impatient, argumentative, cynical, skeptical and contrary." They are also hostile, explosive, lack impulse control, and, sometimes, reckless.

Inevitably, passive-aggressives are envious of the fortunate, the successful, the famous, their superiors, those in favor, and the happy. They vent this venomous jealousy openly and defiantly whenever given the opportunity. But, deep at heart, passive-aggressives are craven. When reprimanded, they immediately revert to begging forgiveness, kowtowing, maudlin protestations, turning on their charm, and promising to behave and perform better in the future.

The Negativistic (Passive-Aggressive) Patient - A Case Study

Disclaimer

The Negativistic (Passive-Aggressive) Personality Disorder appears in Appendix B of the Diagnostic and Statistical Manual (DSM), titled "Criteria Sets and Axes Provided for Further Study."

Notes of first therapy session with Mike, male, 52, diagnosed with Negativistic (Passive-Aggressive) Personality Disorder

Mike is attending therapy at the request of his wife. She complains that he is "emotionally absent" and aloof. Mike shrugs: "We used to have a great marriage, but good things don't last. You can't sustain the same levels of passion and interest throughout the relationship." Isn't his family worth the effort? Another shrug: "It doesn't pay to be a good husband or a good father. Look what my loving wife did to me. In any case, at my age the future is behind me. Carpe Diem is my motto."

Does he consider his wife's demands to be unreasonable? He flares: "With all due respect, that's between me and my spouse." Then why is he wasting his time and mine? "I didn't ask to be here." Did he prepare a list of things he would like to see improved in his family life? He forgot. Can he compile it for our next meeting? Only if nothing more urgent pops up. It would be difficult to continue to work together if he doesn't keep his promises. He understands and he will see what he can do about it (without great conviction).

The problem is, he says, that he regards psychotherapy as a form of con-artistry: "psychotherapists are snake oil salesmen, latter-day witch doctors, only less efficient." He hates to feel cheated or deceived. Does he often feel that way? He laughs dismissively: he is too clever for run-of-the-mill crooks. He is often underestimated by them.

Do other people besides crooks underestimate him? He admits to being unappreciated and underpaid at work. It bothers him. He deserves more than that. Obsequious intellectual midgets rise to the top in every organization, he observes with virulent envy. How does he cope with this discrepancy between the way he perceives himself and the way others, evidently, evaluate him? He ignores such fools. How can one ignore one's co-workers and one's superiors? He doesn't talk to them. In other words, he sulks?

Not always. He sometimes tries to "enlighten and educate" people he deems "worthy". It often gets him into arguments and he has acquired a reputation as a cantankerous curmudgeon but he doesn't care. Is he an impatient or irritable person? "What do you think?" - he counters - "During this session did I ever lose my cool?" Frequently. He half rises from his chair then thinks better of it and settles down. "Do your thing" - he says sullenly and contemptuously - "Let's get it over with."

Return

Narcissistic Couples: The Double Reflection

Two narcissists of the same type (somatic, cerebral, inverted) are bound to be at each other's throat in no time.

Two narcissists of different types can make each other very happy indeed as serve as each other's perfect sources of narcissistic supply.

Question:

Can two narcissists establish a long-term, stable relationship?

Answer:

Two narcissists of the same type (somatic, cerebral, classic, compensatory, inverted, etc.) cannot maintain a stable, long-term full-fledged, and functional relationship.

There are two types of narcissists: the somatic narcissist and the cerebral narcissist. The somatic type relies on his body and sexuality as Sources of Narcissistic Supply. The cerebral narcissist uses his intellect, his intelligence and his professional achievements to obtain the same.

Narcissists are either predominantly cerebral or overwhelmingly somatic. In other words, they either generate their Narcissistic Supply by using their bodies or by flaunting their minds.

The somatic narcissist flashes his sexual conquests, parades his possessions, puts his muscles on ostentatious display, brags about his physical aesthetics or sexual prowess or exploits, is often a health freak and a hypochondriac. The cerebral narcissist is a know-it-all, haughty and intelligent "computer". He uses his awesome intellect, or knowledge (real or pretended) to secure adoration, adulation and admiration. To him, his body and its maintenance are a burden and a distraction.

Both types are autoerotic (psychosexually in love with themselves, with their bodies or with their brains). Both types prefer masturbation to adult, mature, interactive, multi-dimensional and emotion-laden sex.

The cerebral narcissist is often celibate (even when he has a girlfriend or a spouse). He prefers pornography and sexual auto-stimulation to the real thing. The cerebral narcissist is sometimes a latent (hidden, not yet outed) homosexual.

The somatic narcissist uses other people's bodies to masturbate. Sex with him – pyrotechnics and acrobatics aside – is likely to be an impersonal and emotionally alienating and draining experience. The partner is often treated as an object, an extension of the somatic narcissist, a toy, a warm and pulsating vibrator.

It is a mistake to assume type-constancy. In other words, all narcissists are both cerebral and somatic. In each narcissist, one of the types is dominant. So, the narcissist is either largely cerebral – or dominantly somatic. But the other, recessive (manifested less frequently) type, is there. It is lurking, waiting to erupt. The narcissist swings between his dominant type and his recessive type which manifests mainly after a major narcissistic injury or life crisis.

The cerebral narcissist brandishes his brainpower, exhibits his intellectual achievements, basks in the attention given to his mind and to its products. He hates his body and neglects it. It is a nuisance, a burden, a derided appendix, an inconvenience, a punishment. The cerebral narcissist is asexual (rarely has sex, often years apart). He masturbates regularly and very mechanically. His fantasies are homosexual or paedophiliac or tend to objectify his partner (rape, group sex). He stays away from women because he perceives them to be ruthless predators who are out to consume him.

The cerebral narcissist typically goes through a few major life crises. He gets divorced, goes bankrupt, does time in prison, is threatened, harassed and stalked, is often devalued, betrayed, denigrated and insulted. He is prone to all manner of chronic illnesses.

Invariably, following every life crisis, the somatic narcissist in him takes over. The cerebral narcissist suddenly becomes a lascivious lecher. When this happens, he maintains a few relationships – replete with abundant and addictive sex – going simultaneously. He sometimes participates in and initiates group sex and mass orgies. He exercises, loses weight and hones his body into an irresistible proposition.

This outburst of unrestrained, primordial lust wanes in a few months and he settles back into his cerebral ways. No sex, no women, no body.

These total reversals of character stun his mates. His girlfriend or spouse finds it impossible to digest this eerie transformation from the gregarious, darkly handsome, well-built and sexually insatiable person that swept her off her feet – to the bodiless, bookwormish hermit with not an inkling of interest in either sex or other carnal pleasures.

The cerebral narcissist misses his somatic half, but finding a balance is a doomed quest. The satyre that is the somatic narcissist is forever trapped in the intellectual cage of the cerebral one, the Brain.

Thus, if both members of the couple are cerebral narcissists, for instance if both of them are scholars – the resulting competition prevents them from serving as ample Sources of Narcissistic Supply to each other. Finally the mutual admiration society crumbles.

Consumed by the pursuit of their own narcissistic gratification, they have no time or energy or will left to cater to the narcissistic needs of their partner. Moreover, the partner is perceived as a dangerous and vicious contender for a scarce resource: Sources of Narcissistic Supply. This may be less true if the two narcissists work in totally unrelated academic or intellectual fields.

But if the narcissists involved are of different types, if one of them is cerebral and the other one somatic, a long-term partnership based on the mutual provision of Narcissistic Supply can definitely survive.

Example: if one of the narcissists is somatic (uses his/her body as a source of narcissistic gratification) and the other one cerebral (uses his intellect or his professional achievements as such a source), there is nothing to destabilise such collaboration. It is even potentially emotionally rewarding.

The relationship between these two narcissists resembles the one that exists between an artist and his art or a collector and his collection. This can and does change, of course, as the narcissists involved grow older, flabbier and less agile intellectually. The somatic narcissist is also prone to multiple sexual relationships and encounters intended to support his somatic and sexual self-image. These may subject the relationship to fracturing strains. But, all in all, a stable and enduring relationship can – and often does – develop between dissimilar narcissists.

This rule of thumb ("opposites attract") does not apply to classic-inverted pairing. Cerebral narcissists tend to pair with inverted cerebral narcissists who can appreciate their intellectual accomplishments and appropriate them as, vicariously, their own. Similarly, somatic narcissists bond with their inverted-somatic counterparties.

Though content to derive her narcissistic supply from the awed reactions to her intimate partner's achievements, the inverted narcissist – being of the same type – still feels envious and frustrated by her relative obscurity. In the long run, she succumbs to her self-defeating urges and seeks to ruin the fount of her frustration despite the fact that he also serves as her prime source of narcissistic supply.

Return

False Modesty

The narcissist affects and feigns modesty and self-deprecation for two reasons: (1) To insure against the possibility of being accused of lying if and when he is exposed as a fraud and (2) to extract narcissistic supply from his audience.

"(The courtier) should let it seem as if he himself thinks nothing of his accomplishments which, because of his excellence, he makes others think very highly of ... (The courtier participates in such activities as dancing and music performing) making it clear that he neither seeks nor expects any applause. Nor, even though his performance is outstanding, should he let it be thought that he has spent on it much time or trouble."

(Castiglione, The Book of the Courtier)

Question:

I met many narcissists who are modest – even self-effacing. This seems to conflict with your observations. How do you reconcile the two?

Answer:

The "modesty" displayed by narcissists - especially covert, or inverted narcissists - is false. It is mostly and merely verbal. It is couched in flourishing phrases, emphasised to absurdity, repeated unnecessarily – usually to the point of causing gross inconvenience to the listener. The real aim of such behaviour and its subtext are exactly the opposite of common modesty.

It is intended to either aggrandise the narcissist or to protect his grandiosity from scrutiny and possible erosion. Such modest outbursts precede inflated, grandiosity-laden statements made by the narcissist and pertaining to fields of human knowledge and activity in which he is sorely lacking.

Devoid of systematic and methodical education, the narcissist tries to make do with pompous, or aggressive mannerisms, bombastic announcements, and the unnecessary and wrong usage of professional jargon. He attempts to dazzle his surroundings with apparent "brilliance" and to put possible critics on the defence.

Beneath all this he is shallow, ignorant, improvising, and fearful of being exposed as deceitful. The narcissist is a conjurer of verbosity, using sleight of mouth rather than sleight of hand. He is ever possessed by the fear that he is really a petty crook about to be unearthed and reviled by society.

This is a horrible feeling to endure and a taxing, onerous way to live. The narcissist has to protect himself from his own premonitions, from his internal semipternal trial, his guilt, shame, and anxiety. One of the more efficacious defence mechanisms is false modesty.

The narcissist publicly chastises himself for being unfit, unworthy, lacking, not trained and not (formally) schooled, not objective, cognisant of his own shortcomings and vain. This way, if (or, rather, when) exposed he could always say: "But I told you so in the first place, haven't I?" False modesty is, thus an insurance policy. The narcissist "hedges his bets" by placing a side bet on his own fallibility, weakness, deficiencies and proneness to err.

Yet another function is to extract Narcissistic Supply from the listener. By contrasting his own self-deprecation with a brilliant, dazzling display of ingenuity, wit, intellect, knowledge, or beauty – the narcissist aims to secure an adoring, admiring, approving, or applauding protestation from the listener.

The person to whom the falsely modest statement is addressed is expected to vehemently deny the narcissist's claims: "But, really, you are more of an expert than you say!", or "Why did you tell me that you are unable to do (this or that)? Truly, you are very gifted!" "Don't put yourself down so much - you are a generous man!"

The narcissist then shrugs, smirks, blushes and moves uncomfortably from side to side. This was not his intention, he assures his interlocutor. He did not mean to fish for compliments (exactly what he did mean to do). He really does not deserve the praise. But the aim has, thus, been achieved: the Narcissistic Supply has been doled out and avidly consumed. Despite the narcissist's protestations, he feels much better now.

The narcissist is a dilettante and a charlatan. He glosses over complicated subjects and situations in life. He sails through them powered by shallow acquaintance with rapidly acquired verbal and behavioural vocabularies (which he then promptly proceeds to forget).

False modesty is only one of a series of feigned behaviours. The narcissist is a pathological liar, either implicitly or explicitly. His whole existence is a derivative of a False Self, his deceitful invention and its reflections. With false modesty he seeks to involve others in his mind games, to co-opt them, to force them to collaborate while making ultimate use of social conventions of conduct.

The narcissist, above all, is a shrewd manipulator, well-acquainted with human nature and its fault lines. No narcissist will ever admit to it. In this sense, narcissists are really modest.

Return

The Narcissist as Compulsive Giver

"By gifts one makes slaves and by whips one makes dogs"

Proverb of the Inuit of Greenland

"(The) Israeli zoologist Amotz Zahavi (suggested that) (a)ltruistic giving may be an advertisement of dominance and superiority. Anthropologists know it as the Potlach Effect ... Only a genuinely superior individual can afford to advertise the fact by means of a costly gift ... through costly demonstrations of superiority, including ostentatious generosity and public spirited risk taking... (I)f Zahavi is right ... conspicuous generosity (is) a way of buying unfakeably authentic (self-)advertising."

(Richard Dawkins, The God Delusion, pp. 249-251)

There are two types of narcissists: (I) Stingy and mean and (II) compulsive givers. Most narcissists feel abused and exploited when they have to pay money in order to satisfy the needs and wishes of their "nearest" and "dearest".

Not so the compulsive givers.

To all appearances, the compulsive giver is an altruistic, empathic, and caring person. Actually, he or she is a people-pleaser and a codependent. The compulsive giver is trapped in a narrative of his own confabulation: how his nearest and dearest need him because they are poor, young, inexperienced, lacking in intelligence or good looks, and are otherwise inferior to him. Compulsive giving, therefore, involves pathological narcissism.

The ostentatious largesse of codependent compulsive givers is intended to secure the presence and attachment of their "loved" ones and to fend off looming (and, in their mind, inevitable abandonment.) By giving inexorably they aim to foster in the recipient an addictive habit and thus prevent them from leaving.

In reality, it is the compulsive giver who coerces, cajoles, and tempts people around him to avail themselves of his services or money. He forces himself on the recipients of his ostentatious largesse and the beneficiaries of his generosity or magnanimity. He is unable to deny anyone their wishes or a requests, even when these are not explicit or expressed and are mere figments of his own neediness and grandiose imagination.

Inevitably, he develops unrealistic expectations. He feels that people should be immensely grateful to him and that their gratitude should translate into a kind of obsequiousness. Internally, he seethes and rages against the lack of reciprocity he perceives in his relationships with family, friends, and colleagues. He mutely castigates everyone around him for being so ungenerous. To the compulsive giver, giving is perceived as sacrifice and taking is exploitation. Thus, he gives without grace, always with visible strings attached. No wonder he is always frustrated and often aggressive.

In psychological jargon, we would say that the compulsive giver has alloplastic defenses with an external locus of control. This simply means that he relies on input from people around him to regulate his fluctuating sense of self-worth, his precarious self-esteem, and his ever shifting moods. It also means that he blames the world for his failures. He feels imprisoned in a hostile and mystifying universe, entirely unable to influence events, circumstances, and outcomes. He thus avoids assuming responsibility for the consequences of his actions.

Yet, it is important to realize that the compulsive giver cherishes and relishes his self-conferred victimhood and nurtures his grudges by maintaining a meticulous accounting of everything he gives and receives. This mental operation of masochistic bookkeeping is a background process of which the compulsive giver is sometimes unaware. He is likely to vehemently deny such meanness and narrow-mindedness.

The compulsive giver is an artist of projective identification. He manipulates his closest into behaving exactly the way he expects them to. He keeps lying to them and telling them that the act of giving is the only reward he seeks. All the while he secretly yearns for reciprocity. He rejects any attempt to rob him of his sacrificial status - he won't accept gifts or money and he avoids being the recipient or beneficiary of help or compliments. These false asceticism and fake modesty are mere baits. He uses them to prove to himself that his nearest and dearest are nasty ingrates. "If they wanted to (give me a present or help me), they would have insisted" - he bellows triumphantly, his worst fears and suspicions yet again confirmed.

Gradually, people fall into line. They begin to feel that they are the ones who are doing the compulsive giver a favor by succumbing to his endless and overweening charity. "What can we do?" - they sigh - "It means so much to him and he has put so much effort into it! I just couldn't say no." The roles are reversed and everyone is happy: the beneficiaries benefit and the compulsive giver goes on feeling that the world is unjust and people are self-centered exploiters. As he always suspected.

The Narcissist's Relationship with Money

Click HERE to Watch the Video

When the narcissist has money, he can exercise his sadistic urges freely and with little fear of repercussions. Money shields him from life itself, from the outcomes and consequences of his actions; it insulates him warmly and safely, like a benevolent blanket, like a mother's good night kiss. Yes, money is undoubtedly a love substitute and it allows the narcissist to be his ugly, corrupt, and dilapidated self. Money buys the narcissist absolution and his ego-syntonic friendship, forgiveness, and acceptance. With money in the bank, the narcissist feels at ease with himself, free, arrogantly soaring supreme above the contemptible, unwashed masses.

With money lining his proverbial pockets, the narcissist can always find people poorer than him, a cause for great elation coupled with ostentatious disdain and bumptiousness on his part.

The narcissist rarely uses money to buy, corrupt, and intimidate outright. He is more subtle than that. Contrary to common stereotype, the narcissist's avarice seldom devolves into conspicuous consumption. Many narcissists wear 15 year old tattered clothes, have no car, no house, and no property. It is so even when the narcissist can afford better.

Money has little to do with the narcissist's actual physical needs or even with his social interactions. True, the narcissist leverages lucre to acquire status, or to impress others. But most narcissists conceal the true extent of their wealth, hoard it, accumulate it and, like the misers that they are at heart, count it daily and in the dark. Money is the narcissist's licence to sin and to abuse, his permit, a promise and its fulfillment all at once. It unleashes the beast in the narcissist and, with abandon, encourages him - nay, seduces him - to be himself.

Narcissists are not necessarily tight-fisted, though. Many a narcissist spend money on restaurants and trips abroad and books and health products. They buy gifts (though reluctantly and as a maintenance chore). Narcissists addictively gamble and speculate and lose fortunes. The narcissist is insatiable, always wants more, always loses the little that he has. But he does all this not for the love of money, for he does not use it to gratify his self or to cater to his needs. No, he does not crave money, nor care for it. It is the power that it bestows on him that matters: the legitimacy to dare, to flare, to conquer, to oppose, to resist, to taunt, and to torment.

In all his relationships, the narcissist is either the vanquished or the vanquisher; either the haughty master, or an abject slave; either the dominant, or the recessive. The narcissist interacts along the up-down axis, rather than along the left-right one. His world is rigidly hierarchical and abusively stratified. When submissive, he is contemptibly so. When domineering, he is disdainfully so. His life is a pendulum swinging between oppressed and oppressor.

To subjugate another, one must be capricious, unscrupulous, ruthless, obsessive, hateful, vindictive, and penetrating. One must spot the cracks of vulnerability, the crumbling foundations of susceptibility, the pains, the trigger mechanisms, the Pavlovian reactions of hate, and fear, and hope, and anger. Money liberates the narcissist's mind and unleashes his cold empathy. It endows him with the tranquillity, detachment, and incisiveness of a natural scientist.

With his mind free of the quotidian, the narcissist can concentrate on attaining the desired position: on top, dreaded, and shunned - yet obeyed and deferred to. He then proceeds with cool disinterest to unscramble the human jigsaw puzzles, to manipulate their parts, to enjoy their anguish as he exposes their petty misconduct, harps on their failures, compares them to their betters, and mocks their incompetence, hypocrisy, and cupidity. The narcissist cloaks his misdeeds in socially acceptable garb - only to draw the dagger. He casts himself in the role of a brave, incorruptible iconoclast, a fighter for social justice, for a better future, for more efficiency, for good causes, an altruist, or an empathic and selfless benefactor. But it is all about his sadistic urges, really. It is all about death, not life.

Still, antagonizing and alienating potential benefactors is a pleasure that the narcissist cannot afford on an empty purse. When impoverished, he is altruism embodied: the best of friends, the most caring of tutors, a benevolent guide, a lover of humanity, and a fierce fighter against narcissism, sadism, and abuse in all their forms. He adheres, he obeys, he succumbs, he agrees wholeheartedly, he praises, condones, idolizes, and applauds. He is the perfect audience, an admirer and an adulator, a worm and an amoeba: spineless, adaptable in form, slithery flexibility itself. To behave this way for long is unbearable, hence the narcissist's addiction to money (really, to freedom) in all its forms. It is his evolutionary ladder from slime to the sublime and henceforth to mastery.

The Narcissist's Puppets on the Receiving End

Click HERE to Watch the Video

The recipients of the narcissist's tainted and conditional "largesse" similarly equate money with love. Craving the latter, they settle for the former. With so many strings attached to the narcissist's "gifts" they end up entangled and dangling like dysfunctional marionettes, puppets in the narcissist's theatre of the absurd.

The psychodynamic dimensions of money and giving are myriad and crucial to maintaining the victim's precarious inner balance. People embark of great feats of self-deception and cognitive dissonance to justify the sacrifices in self-respect, dignity, and the perception of reality that they have to make in order to remain on the narcissist's good books.

But self-awareness is never far under the surface. Gradually, the human props in the narcissist's staged plays rebel outwardly or inwardly: they become passive-aggressive, bitter, depressed, and paranoid. They feel alienated, dehumanized, objectified, and misunderstood. They seek to free themselves by becoming contumacious and unruly counterdependents – or by clinging to the narcissist and emotionally extorting all others as flaming codependents.

These reactive behavior patters are ingrained and hard to break. They ossify into the moulds in which the narcissist's victims fester and putrefy, writhing in agony, and crumbling whenever the narcissist inflicts on them abuse in its many forms. If they do not extricate themselves in time, these victims gradually acquire many of the traits and behavior patterns of their narcissistic tormentors and form with them a shared psychosis, a mini-cult of domination and subjugation that is mediated via the ubiquitous dollar sign.

Return

The Misanthropic Altruist

"(The) Israeli zoologist Amotz Zahavi (suggested that) (a)ltruistic giving may be an advertisement of dominance and superiority. Anthropologists know it as the Potlach Effect ... Only a genuinely superior individual can afford to advertise the fact by means of a costly gift ... through costly demonstrations of superiority, including ostentatious generosity and public spirited risk taking... (I)f Zahavi is right ... conspicuous generosity (is) a way of buying unfakeably authentic (self-)advertising."

(Richard Dawkins, The God Delusion, pp. 249-251)

Some narcissists are ostentatiously generous – they donate to charity, lavish gifts on their closest, abundantly provide for their nearest and dearest, and, in general, are open-handed and unstintingly benevolent. How can this be reconciled with the pronounced lack of empathy and with the pernicious self-preoccupation that is so typical of narcissists?

The act of giving enhances the narcissist's sense of omnipotence, his fantastic grandiosity, and the contempt he holds for others. It is easy to feel superior to the supplicating recipients of one's largesse. Narcissistic altruism is about exerting control and maintaining it by fostering dependence in the beneficiaries.

But narcissists give for other reasons as well.

The narcissist flaunts his charitable nature as a bait. He impresses others with his selflessness and kindness and thus lures them into his lair, entraps them, and manipulates and brainwashes them into subservient compliance and obsequious collaboration. People are attracted to the narcissist's larger than life posture – only to discover his true personality traits when it is far too late. "Give a little to take a lot" – is the narcissist's creed.

This does not prevent the narcissist from assuming the role of the exploited victim. Narcissists always complain that life and people are unfair to them and that they invest far more than their "share of the profit". The narcissist feels that he is the sacrificial lamb, the scapegoat, and that his relationships are asymmetric and imbalanced. "She gets out of our marriage far more than I do" – is a common refrain. Or: "I do all the work around here – and they get all the perks and benefits!"

Faced with such (mis)perceived injustice – and once the relationship is clinched and the victim is "hooked" – the narcissist tries to minimise his contributions. He regards his input as a contractual maintenance chore and the unpleasant and inevitable price he has to pay for his Narcissistic Supply.

After many years of feeling deprived and wronged, some narcissists lapse into "sadistic generosity" or "sadistic altruism". They use their giving as a weapon to taunt and torment the needy and to humiliate them. In the distorted thinking of the narcissist, donating money gives him the right and license to hurt, chastise, criticise, and berate the recipient. His generosity, feels the narcissist, elevates him to a higher moral ground.

Most narcissists confine their giving to money and material goods. Their munificence is an abusive defence mechanism, intended to avoid real intimacy. Their "big-hearted" charity renders all their relationships – even with their spouses and children – "business-like", structured, limited, minimal, non-emotional, unambiguous, and non-ambivalent. By doling out bounteously, the narcissist "knows where he stands" and does not feel threatened by demands for commitment, emotional investment, empathy, or intimacy.

In the narcissist's wasteland of a life, even his benevolence is spiteful, sadistic, punitive, and distancing.

Return

The Green-Eyed (Envious, Jealous, Spiteful) Narcissist

The New Oxford Dictionary of English defines envy as:

"A feeling of discontented or resentful longing aroused by someone else's possessions, qualities, or luck."

And an earlier version (The Shorter Oxford English Dictionary) adds:

"Mortification and ill-will occasioned by the contemplation of another's superior advantages".

Pathological envy - the second deadly sin - is a compounded emotion. It is brought on by the realization of some lack, deficiency, or inadequacy in oneself. It is the result of unfavourably comparing oneself to others: to their success, their reputation, their possessions, their luck, or their qualities. It is misery and humiliation and impotent rage and a tortuous, slippery path to nowhere. The effort to break the padded walls of this self-visited purgatory often leads to attacks on the perceived source of frustration.

Narcissists envy everyone: spouses, co-workers, colleagues, celebrities, neighbors. Narcissistic parents envy their own children even though they regard them as mere extensions of themselves, instruments of gratification, and sources of narcissistic supply. Frustrated by unrealized fantasies, these mothers and fathers or caretakers charge their offspring with the task of fulfilling these failed dreams and resurrecting the parents' battered False Selves. But when their children succeed in doing this bidding, when they become established or famous, these dysfunctional parents turn on them viciously and virulently, driven by seething and all-consuming envy.

There is a spectrum of reactions to this pernicious and cognitively distorting emotion:

Subsuming the Object of Envy through Imitation

Some narcissists seek to imitate or even emulate their (ever changing) role models. It is as if by imitating the object of his envy, the narcissist BECOMES that object. So, narcissists are likely to adopt their boss' typical gestures, the vocabulary of a successful politician, the views of an esteemed tycoon, even the countenance and actions of the (fictitious) hero of a movie or a novel.

In his pursuit of peace of mind, in his frantic effort to alleviate the burden of consuming jealousy, the narcissist often deteriorates to conspicuous and ostentatious consumption, impulsive and reckless behaviours and substance abuse.

Elsewhere I wrote:

"In extreme cases, to get rich quick through schemes of crime and corruption, to out-wit the system, to prevail is thought by these people to be the epitome of cleverness (providing one does not get caught), the sport of living, a winked-at vice, a spice."

Destroying the Frustrating Object

Other narcissists "choose" to destroy the object that gives them so much grief by provoking in them feelings of inadequacy and frustration. They display obsessive, blind animosity and engage in compulsive acts of rivalry often at the cost of self-destruction and self-isolation.

In my essay "The Dance of Jael", I wrote:

"This hydra has many heads. From scratching the paint of new cars and flattening their tyres, to spreading vicious gossip, to media-hyped arrests of successful and rich businessmen, to wars against advantaged neighbours.

The stifling, condensed vapours of envy cannot be dispersed.

They invade their victims, their rageful eyes, their calculating souls, they guide their hands in evil doings and dip their tongues in vitriol...

(The envious narcissist's existence is) a constant hiss, a tangible malice, the piercing of a thousand eyes. The imminence and immanence of violence.

The poisoned joy of depriving the other of that which you don't or cannot have."

Self-Deprecation

From my essay, "The Dance of Jael":

"There are those narcissists who idealize the successful and the rich and the lucky. They attribute to them super-human, almost divine, qualities...

In an effort to justify the agonizing disparities between themselves and others, they humble themselves as they elevate the others.

They reduce and diminish their own gifts, they disparage their own achievements, they degrade their own possessions and look with disdain and contempt upon their nearest and dearest, who are unable to discern their fundamental shortcomings. They feel worthy only of abasement and punishment. Besieged by guilt and remorse, voided of self-esteem, perpetually self-hating and self-deprecating - this is by far the more dangerous species of narcissist.

For he who derives contentment from his own humiliation cannot but derive happiness from the downfall of others. Indeed, most of them end up driving the objects of their own devotion and adulation to destruction and decrepitude..."

Cognitive Dissonance

"...But the most common reaction is the good old cognitive dissonance. It is to believe that the grapes are sour rather than to admit that they are craved.

These people devalue the source of their frustration and envy. They find faults, unattractive features, high costs to pay, immorality in everything they really most desire and aspire to and in everyone who has attained that which they so often can't. They walk amongst us, critical and self-righteous, inflated with a justice of their making and secure in the wisdom of being what they are rather than what they could have been and really wish to be. They make a virtue of jejune abstention, of wishful constipation, of judgmental neutrality, this oxymoron, the favourite of the disabled."

Avoidance - The Schizoid Solution

And then, of course, there is my favourite solution: avoidance. To witness the success and joy of others is too painful, too high a price to pay. So, I stay at home, alone and incommunicado. I inhabit the artificial bubble that is my world where I am king and country, I am the law and yardstick, I am the one and only. There, in the penumbral recesses of my study, my flickering laptop for company, the only noises are electronic and I am the resident of my own burgeoning delusions. I am happy and soothed. I am what I can dream and dream my very being. I am no longer real, simply a narrative, an invention of my fervent mind, a colourful myth, sustaining and engulfing. I am content.

Romantic Jealousy

Pathological envy is not the same as romantic jealousy. These two emotions have little to do with each other.

Romantic jealousy is the product of a violation of trust; a breach of romantic exclusivity of intimacy; and a denial of possession. It also involves damage to the self-esteem and self-perception of the cuckolded spouse, as he compares himself unfavourably to the "competition": the affair is perceived to be an overall rejection of the cheated partner.

In romantic pairing certain activities are exclusive and, therefore, confer meaning (render the relationship unique and thereby significant.) Sex is the most common of such pursuits, but it could be anything the parties agree on: intimate conversations, travelling together, reading poetry, or skiing. Such activities enhance bonding (generate a mild possessive shared psychosis, really). When one of the partners violates this exclusivity by engaging in the same undertakings with outsiders, the relationship is rendered meaningless ("nonspecial").

But there's much more to it when it comes to narcissists.

Romantic jealousy is a narcissistic defence. It reflects the narcissistic traits and behaviors of possessiveness; objectification (treating the spouse and regarding her as an object); and extension (treating the spouse and regarding her as an extension of oneself: devoid of autonomy, personality, needs, wishes, and emotions). Thus, the spouse's cheating (as in infidelity) is perceived by the narcissist to be tantamount to a violation of and an encroachment on his self, or, more simply put: it amounts to a major narcissistic injury.

Exactly like non-narcissists, narcissists are humiliated by having been lied to; suffer abandonment anxiety; compare themselves with the spouse's new paramour; and feel deprived when the "services" of the unfaithful spouse are no longer available to them (a denial of service which may encompass sex, emotional intimacy, house chores, companionship, or any other function.)

But, in the narcissist, the violation of trust provokes full-scale and raging paranoia (where else lurks deceit?); the breach of exclusivity threatens the aforementioned narcissistic enmeshment; and the denial of possession translates to an overwhelming fear of loss and to crippling abandonment anxiety. Some narcissists even begin to display codependent behaviors, such as clinging, in a desperate attempt to regain their control over the doomed relationship.

Additionally, the narcissist's self-perception as unique, perfect, omnipotent, and omniscient - in short: his False Self - is threatened and challenged by his spouse's affair. If he is, indeed, unique and perfect - why did his spouse stray? If he is omnipotent - how did he fail to prevent the transgression? And if he is omniscient - how come he was the last to know about his wife's fling, or, worse, her long-term illicit liaison?

Narcissists are, consequently, even romantically jealous of intimate partners their spouse has had before the marriage and after the divorce. Some narcissists, realizing that they cannot control their spouses forever, become swingers or engage in group sex, where they feel that, by bringing adultery home, they have "tamed" and "controlled" it. If you can't beat it – join it, as the saying goes.

Return

Shame and Existential Anxiety in Narcissism

The narcissist is guilt-ridden and besieged by shame because reality is incommensurate with his grandiose fantasies, sense of entitlement and his sadistic superego and Ego Ideal:

The introjected voices of parents, peers, and other adult role models in his abusive and traumatized early childhood.

We all have a scenario of our life. We invent, adopt, are led by and measure ourselves against our personal narratives. These are, normally, commensurate with our personal histories, our predilections, our abilities, limitations, and our skills. We are not likely to invent a narrative which is wildly out of synch with our selves.

We rarely judge ourselves by a narrative which is not somehow correlated to what we can reasonably expect to achieve. In other words, we are not likely to frustrate and punish ourselves knowingly. As we grow older, our narrative changes. Parts of it are realized and this increases our self-confidence, sense of self-worth and self-esteem and makes us feel fulfilled, satisfied, and at peace with ourselves.

The narcissist differs from normal people in that his is a ***HIGHLY*** unrealistic personal narrative. This choice could be imposed and inculcated by a sadistic and hateful Primary Object (a narcissistic, domineering mother, for instance) – or it could be the product of the narcissist's own tortured psyche. Instead of realistic expectations of himself, the narcissist has grandiose fantasies. The latter cannot be effectively pursued. They are elusive, ever receding targets.

This constant failure (the Grandiosity Gap) leads to dysphorias (bouts of sadness) and to losses. Observed from the outside, the narcissist is perceived to be odd, prone to illusions and self-delusions and, therefore, lacking in judgement.

The dysphorias – the bitter fruits of the narcissist's impossible demands of himself – are painful. Gradually the narcissist learns to avoid them by eschewing a structured narrative altogether. Life's disappointments and setbacks condition him to understand that his specific "brand" of unrealistic narrative inevitably leads to frustration, sadness and agony and is a form of self-punishment (inflicted on him by his sadistic, rigid Superego).

This incessant punishment serves another purpose: to support and confirm the negative judgement meted out by the narcissist's Primary Objects (usually, by his parents or caregivers) in his early childhood (now, an inseparable part of his Superego).

The narcissist's mother, for instance, may have consistently insisted that the narcissist is bad, rotten, or useless. Surely, she could not have been wrong, goes the narcissist's internal dialog. Even raising the possibility that she may have been wrong proves her right! The narcissist feels compelled to validate her verdict by making sure that he indeed ***BECOMES*** bad, rotten and useless.

Yet, no human being – however deformed – can live without a narrative. The narcissist develops circular, ad-hoc, circumstantial, and fantastic "life-stories" (the Contingent Narratives). Their role is to avoid confrontation with (the often disappointing and disillusioning) reality. He thus reduces the number of dysphorias and their strength, though he usually fails to avoid the Narcissistic Cycle (see FAQ 43).

The narcissist pays a heavy price for accommodating his dysfunctional narratives:

Emptiness, existential loneliness (he shares no common psychic ground with other humans), sadness, drifting, emotional absence, emotional platitude, mechanisation/robotisation (lack of anima, excess persona in Jung's terms) and meaninglessness. This fuels his envy and the resulting rage and amplifies the EIPM (Emotional Involvement Preventive Measures) – see Chapter Eight of the Essay.

The narcissist develop a "Zu Leicht – Zu Schwer" ("Too Easy – Too difficult") syndrome:

On the one hand, the narcissist's life is unbearably difficult. The few real achievements he does have should normally have mitigated this perceived harshness. But, in order to preserve his sense of omnipotence, he is forced to "downgrade" these accomplishments by labelling them as "too easy".

The narcissist cannot admit that he had toiled to achieve something and, with this confession, shatter his grandiose False Self. He must belittle every achievement of his and make it appear to be a routine triviality. This is intended to support the dreamland quality of his fragmented personality. But it also prevents him from deriving the psychological benefits which usually accrue to goal attainment: an enhancement of self-confidence, a more realistic self-assessment of one's capabilities and abilities, a strengthening sense of self-worth.

The narcissist is doomed to roam a circular labyrinth. When he does achieve something – he demotes it in order to enhance his own sense of omnipotence, perfection, and brilliance. When he fails, he dares not face reality. He escapes to the land of no narratives where life is nothing but a meaningless wasteland. The narcissist whiles his life away.

But what is it like being a narcissist?

The narcissist is often anxious. It is usually unconscious, like a nagging pain, a permanence, like being immersed in a gelatinous liquid, trapped and helpless, or as the DSM puts it, narcissism is "all-pervasive". Still, these anxieties are never diffuse. The narcissist worries about specific people, or possible events, or more or less plausible scenarios. He seems to constantly conjure up some reason or another to be worried or offended.

Positive past experiences do not ameliorate this preoccupation. The narcissist believes that the world is hostile, a cruelly arbitrary, ominously contrarian, contrivingly cunning and indifferently crushing place. The narcissist simply "knows" it will all end badly and for no good reason. Life is too good to be true and too bad to endure. Civilization is an ideal and the deviations from it are what we call "history". The narcissist is incurably pessimistic, an ignoramus by choice and incorrigibly blind to any evidence to the contrary.

Underneath all this, there is a Generalised Anxiety. The narcissist fears life and what people do to each other. He fears his fear and what it does to him. He knows that he is a participant in a game whose rules he will never master and in which his very existence is at stake. He trusts no one, believes in nothing, knows only two certainties: evil exists and life is meaningless. He is convinced that no one cares.

This existential angst that permeates his every cell is atavistic and irrational. It has no name or likeness. It is like the monsters in every child's bedroom with the lights turned off. But being the rationalising and intellectualising creatures that cerebral narcissists are – they instantly label this unease, explain it away, analyse it and attempt to predict its onset.

They attribute this poisonous presence to some external cause. They set it in a pattern, embed it in a context, transform it into a link in the great chain of being. Hence, they transform diffuse anxiety into focused worries. Worries are known and measurable quantities. They have reasons which can be tackled and eliminated. They have a beginning and an end. They are linked to names, to places, faces and to people. Worries are human.

Thus, the narcissist transforms his demons into compulsive notations in his real or mental diary: check this, do that, apply preventive measures, do not allow, pursue, attack, avoid. The narcissist ritualizes both his discomfort and his attempts to cope with it.

But such excessive worrying – whose sole intent is to convert irrational anxiety into the mundane and tangible – is the stuff of paranoia.

For what is paranoia if not the attribution of inner disintegration to external persecution, the assignment of malevolent agents from the outside to the figments of turmoil inside? The paranoid seeks to alleviate his own voiding by irrationally clinging to rationality. Things are so bad, he says, mainly to himself, because I am a victim, because "they" are after me and I am hunted by the juggernaut of state, or by the Freemasons, or by the Jews, or by the neighbourhood librarian. This is the path that leads from the cloud of anxiety, through the lamp-posts of worry to the consuming darkness of paranoia.

Paranoia is a defence against anxiety and against aggression. In the paranoid state, the latter is projected outwards, upon imaginary others, the instruments of one's crucifixion.

Anxiety is also a defence against aggressive impulses. Therefore, anxiety and paranoia are sisters, the latter merely a focused form of the former. The mentally disordered defend against their own aggressive propensities by either being anxious or by becoming paranoid.

Yet, aggression has numerous guises, not only anxiety and paranoia. One of its favourite disguises is boredom. Like its relation, depression, boredom is aggression directed inwards. It threatens to drown the bored person in a primordial soup of inaction and energy depletion. It is anhedonic (pleasure depriving) and dysphoric (leads to profound sadness). But it is also threatening, perhaps because it is so reminiscent of death.

Not surprisingly, the narcissist is most worried when bored. The narcissist is aggressive. He channels his aggression and internalises it. He experiences his bottled wrath as boredom.

When the narcissist is bored, he feels threatened by his ennui in a vague, mysterious way. Anxiety ensues. He rushes to construct an intellectual edifice to accommodate all these primitive emotions and their transubstantiations. He identifies reasons, causes, effects and possibilities in the outer world. He builds scenarios. He spins narratives. As a result, he feels no more anxiety. He has identified the enemy (or so he thinks). And now, instead of being anxious, he is simply worried. Or paranoid.

The narcissist often strikes people as "laid back" – or, less charitably: lazy, parasitic, spoiled, and self-indulgent. But, as usual with narcissists, appearances deceive. Narcissists are either compulsively driven over-achievers – or chronic under-achieving wastrels. Most of them fail to make full and productive use of their potential and capacities. Many avoid even the now standard paths of an academic degree, a career, or family life.

The disparity between the accomplishments of the narcissist and his grandiose fantasies and inflated self image – the Grandiosity Gap – is staggering and, in the long run, unsustainable. It imposes onerous exigencies on the narcissist's grasp of reality and on his meagre social skills. It pushes him either to reclusion or to a frenzy of "acquisitions" – cars, women, wealth, power.

Yet, no matter how successful the narcissist is – many of them end up being abject failures – the Grandiosity Gap can never be bridged. The narcissist's False Self is so unrealistic and his Superego so sadistic that there is nothing the narcissist can do to extricate himself from the Kafkaesque trial that is his life.

The narcissist is a slave to his own inertia. Some narcissists are forever accelerating on the way to ever higher peaks and ever greener pastures. Others succumb to numbing routines, the expenditure of minimal energy, and to preying on the vulnerable. But either way, the narcissist's life is out of control, at the mercy of pitiless inner voices and internal forces.

Narcissists are one-state machines, programmed to extract Narcissistic Supply from others. To do so, they develop early on a set of immutable routines. This propensity for repetition, inability to change and rigidity confine the narcissist, stunt his development, and limit his horizons. Add to this his overpowering sense of entitlement, his visceral fear of failure, and his invariable need to both feel unique and be perceived as such – and one often ends up with a recipe for inaction.

The under-achieving narcissist dodges challenges, eludes tests, shirks competition, sidesteps expectations, ducks responsibilities, evades authority – because he is afraid to fail and because doing something everyone else does endangers his sense of uniqueness. Hence the narcissist's apparent "laziness" and "parasitism". His sense of entitlement – with no commensurate accomplishments or investment – irritates his social milieu. People tend to regard such narcissists as "spoiled brats".

In specious contrast, the over-achieving narcissist seeks challenges and risks, provokes competition, embellishes expectations, aggressively bids for responsibilities and authority and seems to be possessed with an eerie self-confidence. People tend to regard such specimen as "entrepreneurial", "daring", "visionary", or "tyrannical". Yet, these narcissists too are mortified by potential failure, driven by a strong conviction of entitlement, and strive to be unique and be perceived as such.

Their hyperactivity is merely the flip side of the under-achiever's inactivity: it is as fallacious and as empty and as doomed to miscarriage and disgrace. It is often sterile or illusory, all smoke and mirrors rather than substance. The precarious "achievements" of such narcissists invariably unravel. They often act outside the law or social norms. Their industriousness, workaholism, ambition, and commitment are intended to disguise their essential inability to produce and build. Theirs is a whistle in the dark, a pretension, a Potemkin life, all make-belief and thunder.

A Comment about Shame

Click HERE to Watch the Video

The Grandiosity Gap is the difference between self-image - the way the narcissist perceives himself - and contravening cues from reality. The greater the conflict between grandiosity and reality, the bigger the gap and the greater the narcissist's feelings of shame and guilt.

There are two varieties of shame:

Narcissistic Shame – which is the narcissist's experience of the Grandiosity Gap (and its affective correlate). Subjectively it is experienced as a pervasive feeling of worthlessness (the dysfunctional regulation of self-worth is the crux of pathological narcissism), "invisibleness" and ridiculousness. The patient feels pathetic and foolish, deserving of mockery and humiliation.

Narcissists adopt all kinds of defences to counter narcissistic shame. They develop addictive, reckless, or impulsive behaviours. They deny, withdraw, rage, or engage in the compulsive pursuit of some kind of (unattainable, of course) perfection. They display haughtiness and exhibitionism and so on. All these defences are primitive and involve splitting, projection, projective identification, and intellectualization.

The second type of shame is *Self-Related*. It is a result of the gap between the narcissist's grandiose Ego Ideal and his Self or Ego. This is a well-known concept of shame and it has been explored widely in the works of Freud [1914], Reich [1960], Jacobson [1964], Kohut [1977], Kingston [1983], Spero [1984] and Morrison [1989].

One must draw a clear distinction between *guilt* (or control)–related shame and *conformity*-related shame.

Guilt is an "objectively" determinable philosophical entity (given relevant knowledge regarding the society and culture in question). It is context-dependent. It is the derivative of an underlying assumption by *OTHERS* that a Moral Agent exerts control over certain aspects of the world. This assumed control by the agent imputes guilt to it, if it acts in a manner incommensurate with prevailing morals, or refrains from acting in a manner commensurate with them.

Shame, in this case, here is an outcome of the *ACTUAL* occurrence of *AVOIDABLE* outcomes - events which impute guilt to a Moral Agent who acted wrongly or refrained from acting.

We must distinguish *GUILT* from *GUILT FEELINGS*, though. Guilt follows events. Guilt feelings can precede them.

Guilt feelings (and the attaching shame) can be *ANTICIPATORY*. Moral Agents assume that they control certain aspects of the world. This makes them able to predict the outcomes of their *INTENTIONS* and feels guilt and shame as a result - even if nothing happened!

Guilt Feelings are composed of a component of Fear and a component of Anxiety. Fear is related to the external, objective, observable consequences of actions or inaction by the Moral Agent. Anxiety has to do with *INNER* consequences. It is ego-dystonic and threatens the identity of the Moral Agent because being Moral is an important part of it. The internalisation of guilt feelings leads to a shame reaction.

Thus, shame has to do with guilty feelings, not with *GUILT*, per se. To reiterate, *guilt* is determined by the reactions and anticipated reactions of others to external outcomes such as avoidable waste or preventable failure (the FEAR component). *Guilty feelings* are the reactions and anticipated reactions of the Moral Agent itself to internal outcomes (helplessness or loss of presumed control, narcissistic injuries – the ANXIETY component).

There is also *conformity-related shame*. It has to do with the narcissist's feeling of "otherness". It similarly involves a component of fear (of the reactions of others to one's otherness) and of anxiety (of the reactions of oneself to one's otherness).

Guilt-related shame is connected to self-related shame (perhaps through a psychic construct akin to the Superego). Conformity-related shame is more akin to narcissistic shame.

Lidija Rangelovska's View of Shame

Lidija Rangelovska advanced the idea that some children subjected to abuse in dysfunctional families – objectified, dehumanized, their boundaries breached, and their growth stunted – develop intense feelings of shame. They turn out to be codependents or narcissists owing to their genetic makeup and innate character. According to her, children who turned out to be codependents as adults are resilient, while the more fragile narcissists seek to evade shame by concocting and then deploying the False Self.

As Lidija Rangelovska observes, shame motivates "normal" people and those suffering from Cluster B personality disorders differently. It constitutes a threat to the former's True Self and to the latter's False Self. Owing to the disparate functionality and psychodynamics of the True and False selves, the ways shame affects behavior and manifests in both populations differ. Additionally, pervasive, constant shame fosters anxiety and even fears or phobias. These can have either an inhibitory effect – or, on the contrary, disinhibitory functions (motivate to action.) Both narcissists and codependents compensate for their shame, the former by developing a "need to be needed" and the latter by developing a "need to deny their neediness".

The True Self involves an accurate reality test with minimal and marginal cognitive deficits as well as the capacity to empathize on all levels, including and especially the emotional level. People whose True Self is intact, mature, and operational are capable of relating to others deeply (for example, by loving them). Their sense of self-worth is stable and grounded in a true and tested assessment of who they are. Maintaining a distinction between what we really are and what we dream of becoming, knowing our limits, our advantages and faults and having a sense of realistic accomplishments in our life are of paramount importance in the establishment and maintenance of our self-esteem, sense of self-worth and self-confidence.

Shame threatens the True Self by challenging the affected person's ego-syntony: by forcing her to "feel bad" about something she has said or done. The solution is usually facile and at hand: reverse the situation by apologizing or by making amends.

In contrast, the False Self leads to false assumptions and to a contorted personal narrative, to a fantastic worldview, and to a grandiose, inflated sense of being. The latter is rarely grounded in real achievements or merit. The narcissist's feeling of entitlement is all-pervasive, demanding and aggressive. It easily deteriorates into the open verbal, psychological and physical abuse of others.

When the patient with the False Self feels shame it is because his grandiosity, the fantastic narrative that underpins his False Self, is challenged, usually - but not necessarily - publicly. There is no easy solution to such a predicament. The situation cannot be reversed and the psychological damage is done. The patient urgently needs to reassert his grandiosity by devaluing or even destroying the frustrating, threatening object, the source of his misery. Another option is to reframe the situation by delusionally ignoring it or recasting it in new terms.

So, while shame motivates normal people to conduct themselves pro-socially and realistically, it pushes the disordered patient in the exact opposite direction: to antisocial or delusional reactions.

Shame is founded on empathy. The normal person empathizes with others. The disordered patient empathizes with himself. But, empathy and shame have little to do with the person with whom we empathize (the empathee). They may simply be the result of conditioning and socialization. In other words, when we hurt someone, we don't experience his or her pain. We experience *our* pain. Hurting somebody - hurts US. The reaction of pain is provoked in *us* by *our* own actions. We have been taught a learned response: to feel pain when we hurt someone.

We attribute feelings, sensations and experiences to the object of our actions. It is the psychological defence mechanism of projection. Unable to conceive of inflicting pain upon ourselves - we displace the source. It is the other's pain that we are feeling, we keep telling ourselves, not our own.

Additionally, we have been taught to feel responsible for our fellow beings and to develop guilt and shame when we fail to do so. So, we also experience pain whenever another person claims to be anguished. We feel guilty owing to his or her condition, we feel somehow accountable even if we had nothing to do with the whole affair. We feel ashamed that we haven't been able to end the other's agony.

Return

Abuse: Covert and Overt

Violence in the family often follows other forms of more subtle and long-term abuse: verbal, emotional, psychological sexual, or financial. It is closely correlated with alcoholism, drug consumption, intimate-partner homicide, teen pregnancy, infant and child mortality, spontaneous abortion, reckless behaviours, suicide, and the onset of mental health disorders.

Most abusers and batterers are males – but a significant minority are women. This being a "Women's Issue", the problem was swept under the carpet for generations and only recently has it come to public awareness. Yet, even today, society – for instance, through the court and the mental health systems – largely ignores domestic violence and abuse in the family. This induces feelings of shame and guilt in the victims and "legitimizes" the role of the abuser.

Violence in the family is mostly spousal – one spouse beating, raping, or otherwise physically harming and torturing the other. But children are also and often victims – either directly, or indirectly. Other vulnerable familial groups include the elderly and the disabled.

Abuse and violence cross geographical and cultural boundaries and social and economic strata. It is common among the rich and the poor, the well-educated and the less so, the young and the middle-aged, city dwellers and rural folk. It is a universal phenomenon.

Abusers exploit, lie, insult, demean, ignore (the "silent treatment"), manipulate, and control.

There are many ways to abuse. To love too much is to abuse. It is tantamount to treating someone as an extension, an object, or an instrument of gratification: one partner is in love with the idea of being in love, of loving someone, anyone - and the other partner is emotionally invested in the idea of being loved by someone, anyone. Both partners are takers, both objectify each other, and both treat each other as mere tools or functions in the fulfilment of their own dreams, expectations, and emotional needs.

To be over-protective, not to respect privacy, to be brutally honest, with a sadistic sense of humour, or consistently tactless – is to abuse. To expect too much, to denigrate, to ignore – are all modes of abuse. There is physical abuse, verbal abuse, psychological abuse, sexual abuse. The list is long. Most abusers abuse surreptitiously. They are "stealth abusers". You have to actually live with one in order to witness the abuse.

There are four important categories of abuse:

Click HERE for *A Classification of Abusive Behaviors*

I. Overt Abuse

The open and explicit abuse of another person. Threatening, coercing, beating, lying, berating, demeaning, chastising, insulting, humiliating, exploiting, ignoring ("silent treatment"), devaluing, unceremoniously discarding, verbal abuse, physical abuse and sexual abuse are all forms of overt abuse.

II. Covert or Controlling Abuse

Abuse is almost entirely about control. It is often a primitive and immature reaction to life circumstances in which the abuser (usually in his childhood) was rendered helpless. It is about re-exerting one's identity, re-establishing predictability, mastering the environment – human and physical.

The bulk of abusive behaviors can be traced to this panicky reaction to the remote potential for loss of control. Many abusers are hypochondriacs (and difficult patients) because they are afraid to lose control over their body, its looks and its proper functioning. They are obsessive-compulsive in an effort to subdue their physical habitat and render it foreseeable. They stalk people and harass them as a means of "being in touch" – another form of control.

To the abuser, nothing exists outside himself. Meaningful others are extensions, internal, assimilated, objects – not external ones. Thus, losing control over a significant other – is equivalent to losing control of a limb, or of one's brain. It is terrifying.

Independent or disobedient people evoke in the abuser the realization that something is wrong with his worldview, that he is not the centre of the world or its cause and that he cannot control what, to him, are internal representations.

To the abuser, losing control means going insane. Because other people are mere elements in the abuser's mind – being unable to manipulate them literally means losing it (his mind). Imagine, if you suddenly were to find out that you cannot manipulate your memories or control your thoughts... Nightmarish!

In his frantic efforts to maintain control or re-assert it, the abuser resorts to a myriad of fiendishly inventive stratagems and mechanisms. Here is a partial list:

Unpredictability and Uncertainty (Intermittent Reinforcement)

The abuser acts unpredictably, capriciously, inconsistently and irrationally. This serves to render others dependent upon the next twist and turn of the abuser, his next inexplicable whim, upon his next outburst, denial, or smile. Withholding (of sex, affection, care, and empathy) and other passive-aggressive behaviors (such as "silent treatment") are integral to this variant of abusive conduct.

The abuser makes sure that **HE** is the only reliable element in the lives of his nearest and dearest – by shattering the rest of their world through his seemingly insane behaviour. He perpetuates his stable presence in their lives – by destabilizing their own.

TIP

Refuse to accept such behaviour. Demand reasonably predictable and rational actions and reactions. Insist on respect for your boundaries, predilections, preferences, and priorities.

Disproportional Reactions

One of the favourite tools of manipulation in the abuser's arsenal is the disproportionality of his reactions. He reacts with supreme rage to the slightest slight. Or, he would punish severely for what he perceives to be an offence against him, no matter how minor. Or, he would throw a temper tantrum over any discord or disagreement, however gently and considerately expressed. Or, he would act inordinately attentive, charming and tempting (even over-sexed, if need be).

This ever-shifting code of conduct and the unusually harsh and arbitrarily applied penalties are premeditated. The victims are kept in the dark. Neediness and dependence on the source of "justice" meted and judgment passed – on the abuser – are thus guaranteed.

TIP

Demand a just and proportional treatment. Reject or ignore unjust and capricious behaviour.

If you are up to the inevitable confrontation, react in kind. Let him taste some of his own medicine.

Dehumanization and Objectification (Abuse)

People have a need to believe in the empathic skills and basic good-heartedness of others. By dehumanizing and objectifying people – the abuser attacks the very foundations of human interaction. This is the "alien" aspect of abusers – they may be excellent imitations of fully formed adults but they are emotionally absent and immature.

Abuse is so horrid, so repulsive, so phantasmagoric – that people recoil in terror. It is then, with their defences absolutely down, that they are the most susceptible and vulnerable to the abuser's control. Physical, psychological, verbal and sexual abuse are all forms of dehumanization and objectification.

TIP

Never show your abuser that you are afraid of him. Do not negotiate with bullies. They are insatiable. Do not succumb to blackmail.

If things get rough – disengage, involve law enforcement officers, friends and colleagues, or threaten him (legally).

Do not keep your abuse a secret. Secrecy is the abuser's weapon.

Never give him a second chance. React with your full arsenal to the first transgression.

Abuse of Information

From the first moments of an encounter with another person, the abuser is on the prowl. He collects information. The more he knows about his potential victim – the better able he is to coerce, manipulate, charm, extort or convert it "to the cause". The abuser does not hesitate to misuse the information he gleaned, regardless of its intimate nature or the circumstances in which he obtained it. This is a powerful tool in his armory.

TIP

Be guarded. Don't be too forthcoming in a first or casual meeting. Gather intelligence.

Be yourself. Don't misrepresent your wishes, boundaries, preferences, priorities, and red lines.

Do not behave inconsistently. Do not go back on your word. Be firm and resolute.

Impossible Situations

The abuser engineers impossible, dangerous, unpredictable, unprecedented, or highly specific situations in which he is sorely needed. The abuser makes sure that his knowledge, his skills, his connections, his sexuality, or his traits are the only ones applicable and the most useful in the situations that he, himself, wrought. The abuser generates his own indispensability.

TIP

Stay away from such quagmires. Scrutinize every offer and suggestion, no matter how innocuous.

Prepare backup plans. Keep others informed of your whereabouts and appraised of your situation.

Be vigilant and doubting. Do not be gullible and suggestible. Better safe than sorry.

III. Control and Abuse by Proxy

If all else fails, the abuser recruits friends, colleagues, mates, family members, the authorities, institutions, neighbours, the media, teachers – in short, third parties – to do his bidding. He uses them to cajole, coerce, threaten, stalk, offer, retreat, tempt, convince, harass, communicate and otherwise manipulate his target. He controls these unaware instruments exactly as he plans to control his ultimate prey. He employs the same mechanisms and devices. And he dumps his props unceremoniously when the job is done.

Another form of control by proxy is to engineer situations in which abuse is inflicted upon another person. Such carefully crafted scenarios of embarrassment and humiliation provoke social sanctions (condemnation, opprobrium, or even physical punishment) against the victim. Society or a social group become the instruments of the abuser.

Triangulation is the coerced introduction of a third party into a relationship, either in the role of a go-between (bridge) or in order to abuse by proxy (of which marital infidelity is one form.) A three-way arrangement is always unstable. In such an environment, the narcissist or psychopath is desirable and indispensable because he appears to keep all his options open (for instance, romantically, with the third party.)

TIP

Often the abuser's proxies are unaware of their role. Expose him. Inform them. Demonstrate to them how they are being abused, misused, and plain used by the abuser.

Trap your abuser. Treat him as he treats you. Involve others. Bring it into the open. Nothing like sunshine to disinfest abuse.

IV. Ambient Abuse and Gaslighting

The fostering, propagation and enhancement of an atmosphere of fear, intimidation, instability, unpredictability and irritation. There are no acts of traceable explicit abuse, nor any manipulative settings of control. Yet, the irksome feeling remains, a disagreeable foreboding, a premonition, a bad omen. This is sometimes called "gaslighting".

In the long term, such an environment erodes the victim's sense of self-worth and self-esteem. Self-confidence is shaken badly. Often, the victim adopts a paranoid or schizoid stance and thus renders himself or herself exposed even more to criticism and judgment. The roles are thus reversed: the victim is considered mentally deranged and the abuser – the suffering soul.

TIP

Run! Get away! Ambient abuse often develops to overt and violent abuse.

You don't owe anyone an explanation - but you owe yourself a life. Bail out.

Continue ...

APPENDIX: A Classification of Abusive Behaviors

Abusive conduct is not a uniform, homogeneous phenomenon. It stems and emanates from multiples sources and manifests in a myriad ways. Following are a few useful distinctions which pertain to abuse and could serve as organizing, taxonomical principles (dimensional typologies) in a kind of matrix.

1. Overt vs. Covert abuse

Overt abuse is the open and explicit, easily discernible, clear-cut abuse of another person in any way, shape, or form (verbal, physical, sexual, financial, psychological-emotional, etc.).

Covert abuse revolves around the abuser's need to assert and maintain control over his victim. It can wear many forms, not all of which are self-evident, unequivocal, and unambiguous.

2. Explicit vs. Stealth or Ambient abuse (Gaslighting)

A more useful distinction, therefore, is between explicit (manifest, obvious, indisputable, easily observable even by a casual spectator or interlocutor) and stealth (or ambient) abuse, also known as gaslighting. This is the fostering, propagation and enhancement of an atmosphere of fear, intimidation, instability, unpredictability and irritation. There are no acts of traceable explicit abuse, nor any manipulative settings of control.

3. Projective vs. Directional abuse

Projective abuse is the outcome of the abuser's projection defense mechanism. Projection is when the abuser attributes to others feelings and traits and motives that he possesses but deems unacceptable, discomfiting, and ill-fitting. This way he disowns these discordant features and secures the right to criticize and chastise others for having or displaying them. Such abuse is often cathartic (see the next pair of categories).

Directional abuse is not the result of projection. It is a set of behaviors aimed at a target (the victim) for the purpose of humiliating, punishing, or manipulating her. Such abusive conduct is functional, geared towards securing a favored and desired outcome.

4. Cathartic vs. Functional abuse

While pair number (3) above deals with the psychodynamic roots of the abuser's misbehavior, the current pair of categories is concerned with its consequences. Some abusers behave the way they do because it alleviates their anxieties; enhances their inflated, grandiose self-image; or purges "impurities" and imperfections that they perceive either in the victim, or in the situation (e.g., in their marriage). Thus, such abuse is cathartic: it is aimed at making the abuser feel better. Projective abuse, for instance, is always cathartic.

The other reason to abuse someone is because the abuser wants to motivate his victim to do something, to feel in a certain way, or to refrain from committing an act. This is functional abuse in that it helps the abuser to adapt to his environment and operate in it, however dysfunctionally.

5. Pattern (or structured) vs. Stochastic (or Random) abuse

Some abusers heap abuse all the time on everyone around them: spouse, children, neighbors, friends, bosses, colleagues, authority figures, and underlings. Abusive conduct is the only way they know how to react to a world which they perceive to be hostile and exploitative. Their behaviors are "hard-wired", rigid, ritualistic, and structured.

Other abusers are less predictable. They are explosive and impulsive. They have a problem with managing their anger. They respond with temper tantrums to narcissistic injuries and real and imaginary slights (ideas of reference). These abusers appear to strike "out of the blue", in a chaotic and random manner.

6. Monovalent vs. Polyvalent abuse

The monovalent abuser abuses only one party, repeatedly, viciously, and thoroughly. Such abusers perpetrate their acts in well-defined locations or frameworks (e.g., at home, or in the workplace). They take great care to hide their hideous exploits and present a socially-acceptable face (or, rather, facade) in public. Their are driven by the need to annihilate the object of their maltreatment, or the source of their frustration and pathological envy.

In contrast, the polyvalent abuser casts his net wide and far and does not "discriminate" in choosing his prey. He is an "equal opportunity abuser" with multiple victims, who, often, have little in common. He is rarely concerned with appearances and regards himself above the Law. He holds everyone - and especially authority figures - in contempt. He is usually antisocial (psychopathic) and narcissistic.

7. Characteristic (personal style) vs. Atypical abuse

Abuse amounts to the personal style of most Pattern, or Structured abusers (see point 5 above). Demeaning, injurious, humiliating, and offensive behavior is their modus operandi, their reflexive reaction to stimuli, and their credo. Stochastic, or Random abusers act normatively and "normally" most of the time. Their abusive conduct is an aberration, a deviation, and perceived by their nearest and dearest to be atypical and even shocking.

8. Normative vs. Deviant abuse.

We all inflict abuse on others from time to time. Some abusive reactions are within the social norms and not considered to be indicative or a personal pathology, or of a socio-cultural anomie. In certain circumstances, abuse as a reaction is called for and deemed healthy and socially-commendable.
Still, the vast majority of abusive behaviors should be regarded as deviant, pathological, antisocial, and perverse.

It is important to distinguish between normative and deviant abuse. A total lack of aggression is as unhealthy as a surfeit. The cultural context is critical in assessing when someone crosses the line and becomes an abuser.

Financial Abuse (Interview granted to the Guardian, June 29, 2013)

Q. Would narcissists often try to restrict their partner's independence by reducing their access to shared family finances? Why?

A. Narcissists are control freaks, paranoid, jealous, possessive, and envious. They are the sad products of early childhood abandonment by parents, caregivers, role models, and/or peers. Hence their extreme abandonment anxiety and insecure attachment style. Fostering financial dependence in their nearest and dearest is just another way of making sure of their continued presence as sources of narcissistic supply (attention.) He who holds the purse strings holds the heart's strings.

Reducing other people to begging and cajoling also buttresses the narcissist's grandiose fantasy of omnipotence and provides him with a somewhat sadistic gratification.

Q. Would it also happen with female narcissists exercising control over men?

A. Yes. There is no major psychodynamic difference between male and female narcissists.

Q. What advice would you give to someone in a relationship with a narcissist? Should they try to keep their finances separate?

A. They should never allow themselves to be irrevocably separated from their family of origin and close friends. They should maintain their support network and refuse to become a part of the narcissist's cult-like shared psychosis. They should make sure that they have independent sources of wealth (a trust fund; real estate; bank accounts; deposits; securities) and sustainable sources of income (a job; rental income; interest and dividends; royalties).

Above all: they should not share with their narcissistic intimate partner the full, unmitigated details of their life and critical bits of information such as banking passwords and safe box access codes.

Q. I understand that narcissists will sometimes sacrifice their finances and get into big trouble financially (even going bankrupt) in order to satisfy other narcissistic desires - so I presume this means that narcissists are also people whose finances can be instable?

A. It is not as simple as that. The classic narcissist maintains an island of stability in his life (e.g.: his job, business, and finances) while the other dimensions of his existence (e.g., interpersonal relations) wallow in chaos and unpredictability. The narcissist may marry, divorce, and remarry with dizzying speed. Everything in his life may be in constant flux: friends, emotions, judgements, values, beliefs, place of residence, affiliations, hobbies. Everything, that is, except his work.

His career is the island of compensating stability in his otherwise mercurial existence. This kind of narcissist is dogged by unmitigated ambition and devotion. He perseveres in one workplace or one job, patiently, persistently and blindly climbing up the corporate ladder and treading the career path. In his pursuit of job fulfilment and achievements, the narcissist is ruthless and unscrupulous – and, very often, successful.

The borderline narcissist reacts to instability in one area of his life by introducing chaos into all the others. Thus, if such a narcissist resigns (or, more likely, is made redundant) – he also relocates to another city or country. If he divorces, he is also likely to resign his job.

This added instability gives this type of narcissist the feeling that all the dimensions of his life are changing simultaneously, that he is being "unshackled", that a transformation is in progress. This, of course, is an illusion. Those who know the narcissist, no longer trust his frequent "conversions", "decisions", "crises", "transformations", "developments" and "periods". They see through his pretensions, protestations, and solemn declarations into the core of his instability. They know that he is not to be relied upon. They know that with narcissists, temporariness is the only permanence.

Narcissists hate routine. When a narcissist finds himself doing the same things over and over again, he gets depressed. He oversleeps, over-eats, over-drinks and, in general, engages in addictive, impulsive, reckless, and compulsive behaviours. This is his way of re-introducing risk and excitement into what he (emotionally) perceives to be a barren life.

The problem is that even the most exciting and varied existence becomes routine after a while. Living in the same country or apartment, meeting the same people, doing essentially the same things (even with changing content) – all "qualify", in the eyes of the narcissist, as stultifying rote.

The narcissist feels entitled. He feels it is his right – due to his intellectual or physical superiority – to lead a thrilling, rewarding, kaleidoscopic life. He wants to force life itself, or at least people around him, to yield to his wishes and needs, supreme among them the need for stimulating variety.

Return

About the Author

About the Author

Sam Vaknin (http://samvak.tripod.com) is the author of Malignant Self-Love: Narcissism Revisited and After the Rain - How the West Lost the East, as well as many other books and ebooks about topics in psychology, relationships, philosophy, economics, and international affairs.

He is the former Editor-in-Chief of Global Politician and served as a columnist for Central Europe Review, PopMatters, eBookWeb , and Bellaonline, and as a United Press International (UPI) Senior Business Correspondent. He was the editor of mental health and Central East Europe categories in The Open Directory and Suite101.

Visit Sam's Web site at http://www.narcissistic-abuse.com

A Personal Word: My Work on Narcissism

I am the author of Malignant Self-love: Narcissism Revisited, the pioneering work about narcissistic abuse, now in its 10th , DSM-V compatible revision. My work is quoted in well over 1000 scholarly publications and in over 3000 books (partial list here). **My Narcissists, Psychopaths, and Abuse YouTube channel and my other channels have more than 18.1 million views and 80,000 subscribers.**

The Web site "Malignant Self-love: Narcissism Revisited" had been, for many years, an Open Directory Cool Site and is a Psych-UK recommended Site.

I am *not a mental health professional* though I am certified in psychological counseling techniques by Brainbench.

I served as the editor of Mental Health Disorders categories in the Open Directory Project and on Mentalhelp.net. I maintain my own Websites about the Narcissistic Personality Disorder (NPD) and about relationships with abusive narcissists and psychopaths here and in HealthyPlace.

You can read my work on many other Web sites: Mental Health Matters, Mental Health Sanctuary, Mental Health Today, Kathi's Mental Health Review and others. I write a column for Bellaonline on Narcissism and Abusive Relationships and am a frequent contributor to Websites such as Self-growth.com and Bizymoms (where I am an expert on personality disorders).

I served as the author of the Personality Disorders topic, Narcissistic Personality Disorder topic, the Verbal and Emotional Abuse topic, and the Spousal Abuse and Domestic Violence topic, all four on Suite101. I am the moderator of the Narcissistic Abuse Study List , the Toxic Relationships Study List, and other mailing lists with a total of c. 20,000 members. I also publish a bi-weekly <u>Abusive Relationships Newsletter</u>. You can view my biography <u>here</u>.

THE AUTHOR

Shmuel (Sam) Vaknin

Curriculum Vitae

Born in 1961 in Qiryat-Yam, Israel

Served in the Israeli Defence Force (1979-1982) in training and education units

Full proficiency in Hebrew and in English

Education

1970 to 1978

Completed nine semesters in the Technion – Israel Institute of Technology, Haifa

1982 to 1983

Ph.D. in Philosophy (dissertation: "Time Asymmetry Revisited") – California Miramar University (formerly: Pacific Western University), California, USA

1982 to 1985

Graduate of numerous courses in Finance Theory and International Trading in the UK and USA.

Certified E-Commerce Concepts Analyst by Brainbench

Certified Financial Analyst by Brainbench

Certified in Psychological Counselling Techniques by Brainbench

Business Experience

1979 to 1983

Commentator in Yedioth Aharonot, Ma'ariv, and Bamakhane. Published sci-fi short fiction in Fantasy 2000.

Founder and co-owner of a chain of computerized information kiosks in Tel-Aviv, Israel.

1982 to 1985

Senior positions with the Nessim D. Gaon Group of Companies in Geneva, Paris and New-York (NOGA and APROFIM SA):

– Chief Analyst of Edible Commodities in the Group's Headquarters in Switzerland

– Manager of the Research and Analysis Division

– Manager of the Data Processing Division

– Project Manager of the Nigerian Computerized Census

– Vice President in charge of RND and Advanced Technologies

– Vice President in charge of Sovereign Debt Financing

1985 to 1986

Represented Canadian Venture Capital Funds in Israel

1986 to 1987

General Manager of IPE Ltd. in London. The firm financed international multi-lateral countertrade and leasing transactions.

1988 to 1990

Co-founder and Director of "Mikbats-Tesuah", a portfolio management firm based in Tel-Aviv.

Activities included large-scale portfolio management, underwriting, forex trading and general financial advisory services.

1990 to Present

Freelance consultant to many of Israel's Blue-Chip firms, mainly on issues related to the capital markets in Israel, Canada, the UK and the USA.

Consultant to foreign RND ventures and to Governments on macro-economic matters.

Freelance journalist in various media in the United States.

1990 to 1995

President of the Israel chapter of the Professors World Peace Academy (PWPA) and (briefly) Israel representative of the "Washington Times".

1993 to 1994

Co-owner and Director of many business enterprises:

– The Omega and Energy Air-conditioning Concern

– AVP Financial Consultants

– Handiman Legal Services – Total annual turnover of the group: 10 million USD.

Co-owner, Director and Finance Manager of COSTI Ltd. – Israel's largest computerized information vendor and developer. Raised funds through a series of private placements locally in the USA, Canada and London.

1993 to 1996

Publisher and Editor of a Capital Markets Newsletter distributed by subscription only to dozens of subscribers countrywide.

Tried and incarcerated for 11 months for his role in an attempted takeover of Israel's Agriculture Bank involving securities fraud.

Managed the Internet and International News Department of an Israeli mass media group, "Ha-Tikshoret and Namer".

Assistant in the Law Faculty in Tel-Aviv University (to Prof. S.G. Shoham)

1996 to 1999

Financial consultant to leading businesses in Macedonia, Russia and the Czech Republic.

Economic commentator in "Nova Makedonija", "Dnevnik", "Makedonija Denes", "Izvestia", "Argumenti i Fakti", "The Middle East Times", "The New Presence", "Central Europe Review", and other periodicals, and in the economic programs on various channels of Macedonian Television.

Chief Lecturer in courses in Macedonia organized by the Agency of Privatization, by the Stock Exchange, and by the Ministry of Trade.

1999 to 2002

Economic Advisor to the Government of the Republic of Macedonia and to the Ministry of Finance.

2001 to 2003

Senior Business Correspondent for United Press International (UPI)

2005 to Present

Associate Editor and columnist, Global Politician

Founding Analyst, The Analyst Network

Contributing Writer, The American Chronicle Media Group

Expert, Self-growth and Bizymoms and contributor to Mental Health Matters

2007 to 2008

Columnist and analyst in "Nova Makedonija", "Fokus", and "Kapital" (Macedonian papers and newsweeklies)

2008 to 2011

Member of the Steering Committee for the Advancement of Healthcare in the Republic of Macedonia

Advisor to the Minister of Health of Macedonia

Seminars and lectures on economic issues in various forums in Macedonia

Contributor to CommentVision

2011 to Present

Editor in Chief of Global Politician and Investment Politics

Columnist in Dnevnik and Publika, Fokus, and Nova Makedonija (Macedonia)

Columnist in InfoPlus and Libertas

Member CFACT Board of Advisors

Contributor to Recovering the Self

Columnist in New York Daily Sun

Teaches at CIAPS (Center for International and Advanced Professional Studies)

2017-8

Visiting Professor of Psychology in Southern Federal University, Rostov-on-Don, Russia

Web and Journalistic Activities

Author of extensive Web sites in:

– Psychology ("Malignant Self-love: Narcissism Revisited") – an Open Directory Cool Site for 8 years

– Philosophy ("Philosophical Musings")

– Economics and Geopolitics ("World in Conflict and Transition")

Owner of the Narcissistic Abuse Study List, the Toxic Relationships List, and the Abusive Relationships Newsletter (more than 7,000 members)

Owner of the Economies in Conflict and Transition Study List and the Links and Factoid Study List

Editor of mental health disorders and Central and Eastern Europe categories in various Web directories (Open Directory, Search Europe, Mentalhelp.net)

Editor of the Personality Disorders, Narcissistic Personality Disorder, the Verbal and Emotional Abuse, and the Spousal (Domestic) Abuse and Violence topics on Suite 101 and contributing author on Bellaonline.

Columnist and commentator in "The New Presence", United Press International (UPI), InternetContent, eBookWeb, PopMatters, Global Politician, The Analyst Network, Conservative Voice, The American Chronicle Media Group, eBookNet.org, and "Central Europe Review".

Publications and Awards

"Managing Investment Portfolios in States of Uncertainty", Limon Publishers, Tel-Aviv, 1988

"The Gambling Industry", Limon Publishers, Tel-Aviv, 1990

"Requesting My Loved One: Short Stories", Miskal-Yedioth Aharonot, Tel-Aviv, 1997

"The Suffering of Being Kafka" (electronic book of Hebrew and English Short Fiction), Prague, 1998-2004

"The Macedonian Economy at a Crossroads – On the Way to a Healthier Economy" (dialogues with Nikola Gruevski), Skopje, 1998

"The Exporter's Pocketbook" Ministry of Trade, Republic of Macedonia, Skopje, 1999

"Malignant Self-love: Narcissism Revisited", Narcissus Publications, Prague and Skopje, 1999-2015 (Read excerpts – click here)

The Narcissism, Psychopathy, and Abuse in Relationships Series (electronic books regarding relationships with abusive narcissists and psychopaths), Prague, 1999-2015

"After the Rain – How the West Lost the East", Narcissus Publications in association with Central Europe Review/CEENMI, Prague and Skopje, 2000

Personality Disorders Revisited (electronic book about personality disorders), Prague, 2007

More than 30 e-books about psychology, international affairs, business and economics, philosophy, short fiction, and reference (free downloads here)

Winner of numerous awards, among them Israel's Council of Culture and Art Prize for Maiden Prose (1997), The Rotary Club Award for Social Studies (1976), and the Bilateral Relations Studies Award of the American Embassy in Israel (1978).

Hundreds of professional articles in all fields of finance and economics, and numerous articles dealing with geopolitical and political economic issues, published in both print and Web periodicals in many countries.

Many appearances in the electronic and print media on subjects in psychology, philosophy, and the sciences, and concerning economic matters.

Citations via Google Scholar page

Write to Me:

samvaknin@gmail.com

narcissisticabuse-owner@yahoogroups.com

My Web Sites

Economy/Politics:

http://ceeandbalkan.tripod.com/

Psychology:

http://www.narcissistic-abuse.com/

Philosophy:

http://philosophos.tripod.com/

Poetry:

http://samvak.tripod.com/contents.html

Fiction:

http://samvak.tripod.com/sipurim.html

Participate in discussions about Abusive Relationships:

https://plus.google.com/communities/116582645889927140499

http://www.runboard.com/bnarcissisticabuserecovery

http://thepsychopath.freeforums.org/

The Narcissistic Abuse Study List

http://health.groups.yahoo.com/group/narcissisticabuse/

The Toxic Relationships Study List

http://groups.yahoo.com/group/toxicrelationships

Abusive Relationships Newsletter

http://groups.google.com/group/narcissisticabuse/

Follow my work on NARCISSISTS and PSYCHOPATHS

As well as international affairs and economics

http://www.narcissistic-abuse.com/mediakit.html

(Sam Vaknin's Media Kit and Press Room)

Be my friend on **Facebook**:

http://www.facebook.com/samvaknin

Subscribe to my **YouTube** channel (hundreds of videos about narcissists and psychopaths and abuse in relationships):

http://www.youtube.com/samvaknin

Read my **Blog**:

http://narcissistpsychopathabuse.blogspot.mk

http://narcissistpsychopathabuse.blogspot.com

Subscribe to my other **YouTube** channel (100+ videos about international affairs, economics, and philosophy):

http://www.youtube.com/vakninmusings

Subscribe to my **YouTube** channel Vaknin Says:

http://www.youtube.com/vakninsays

You may also with to join **Malignant Self-love: Narcissism Revisited**
On **Facebook** and **Google Plus**:

http://www.facebook.com/pages/Malignant-Self-Love-Narcissism-Revisited/50634038043 or

https://www.facebook.com/NarcissusPublications

http://www.facebook.com/narcissistpsychopathabuse

https://plus.google.com/u/0/111189140058482892878/posts

Follow me on **Twitter**, **MySpace**, **Google Plus**, **Pinterest**, **Tumblr**, **Ello, Linkedin**, or **Instagram**:

https://www.instagram.com/vakninsamnarcissist/

http://pinterest.com/samvaknin/the-psychopathic-narcissist-and-his-world/

http://www.twitter.com/samvaknin

https://www.minds.com/samvaknin

http://www.myspace.com/samvaknin

https://plus.google.com/115041965408538110094

http://narcissistpsychopath-abuse.tumblr.com/

http://www.linkedin.com/in/samvaknin

https://ello.co/malignantselflove

https://ello.co/samvaknin

Subscribe to my **Scribd** page: dozens of books for download at no charge to you!

http://www.scribd.com/samvaknin

Zadanliran is following my work as well:

Abused? Stalked? Harassed? Bullied? Victimized?
Afraid? Confused? Need HELP? DO SOMETHING ABOUT IT!

Brought up by a Narcissistic Parent?

Married to a Narcissist – or Divorcing One?

Afraid your Children will turn out to be the same?

Want to cope with this pernicious, baffling condition?

OR

Are You a Narcissist – or suspect that you are one…

These books and video lectures will teach you how to…

Cope, Survive, and Protect Your Loved Ones!

We offer you three types of products:

I. **"Malignant Self-love: Narcissism Revisited"** (the print edition) via Barnes and Noble, directly from the publisher, or via Amazon;

II. **E-books** (electronic files to be read on a computer, laptop, Nook, or Kindle e-reader devices, or smartphone); and

III. **DVDs** with video lectures.

I. PRINT EDITION

Copies **signed** and **dedicated** by the Author, Sam Vaknin (use only this link!):
http://www.amazon.com/gp/product/8023833847/ ref=cm_sw_r_tw_myi?m=A2IY3GUWWKHV9B

1. From BARNES and NOBLE

You can buy the PRINT edition of "Malignant Self-love: Narcissism Revisited" (March 2015) from Barnes and Noble (the cheapest option, but does not include a bonus pack):
http://search.barnesandnoble.com/bookSearch/isbnInquiry.asp?r=1&ISBN=9788023833843

Or, click on this link – http://www.bn.com – and search for "Sam Vaknin" or "Malignant Self-love".

2. From the PUBLISHER

"Malignant Self-love: Narcissism Revisited" is now available also from the publisher (more expensive, but includes a bonus pack):
More information:
http://www.narcissistic-abuse.com/thebook.html

3. From AMAZON.COM

To purchase from Amazon – click on these links:

https://www.amazon.com/dp/1983208175 (US)

https://www.amazon.co.uk/dp/1983208175 (UK)

http://www.amazon.com/Malignant-Self-Love-Narcissism-Sam-Vaknin/dp/8023833847

II. ELECTRONIC BOOKS (e-Books)

From KINDLE (AMAZON)

Kindle Books about Narcissists, Psychopaths, and Abusive Relationships – click on these links:

http://www.amazon.com/s/ref=ntt_athr_dp_sr_1?_encoding=UTF8&field-author=Sam%20Vaknin&search-alias=digital-text&sort=relevancerank (Amazon USA)

http://www.amazon.co.uk/s/ref=ntt_athr_dp_sr_1?_encoding=UTF8&field-author=Sam%20Vaknin&search-alias=digital-text&sort=relevancerank (Amazon UK)

1. "Malignant Self-love: Narcissism Revisited"

TENTH, Revised Edition (2015) – FULL TEXT

https://www.amazon.com/Malignant-Self-love-Narcissism-Revisited-FULL-ebook/dp/B00HDJF7HC/

https://www.amazon.co.uk/Malignant-Self-love-Narcissism-Revisited-FULL-ebook/dp/B00HDJF7HC/

2. "The Narcissist and Psychopath in the Workplace"

https://www.amazon.com/dp/B00708XMSC

3. "Abusive Relationships WORKBOOK"

https://www.amazon.com/dp/B00709FRMU

4. "Toxic Relationships: Abuse and its Aftermath"

https://www.amazon.com/dp/B00708XL5G

5. "The Narcissist and Psychopath in Therapy"

https://www.amazon.com/dp/B00708NLXI

6. "Pathological Narcissism FAQs (Frequently Asked Questions)"

https://www.amazon.com/dp/B007093HIG

7. "The World of the Narcissist"

https://www.amazon.com/dp/B0070956N0

8. "Excerpts from the Archives of the Narcissism List"

https://www.amazon.com/dp/B007097R7S

9. "Diary of a Narcissist"

https://www.amazon.com/dp/B00709CDA4

NEW!!! "A to Z of Narcissistic Abuse, Narcissism, and Narcissistic Personality Disorder Encyclopedia: The Narcissism Bible"

Almost 1000 pages of A to Z entries: the first comprehensive encyclopedia of pathological narcissism and Narcissistic Personality Disorder in clinical and non-clinical settings; family, workplace, church, community, law enforcement and judiciary, and politics.

Click on this link to purchase the e-book:

https://www.amazon.com/Narcissistic-Abuse-Narcissism-Personality-Encyclopedia-ebook/dp/B00POZ0I1C

NEW!!! "Personality Disorders Revisited"

450 pages about Borderline, Narcissistic, Antisocial-Psychopathic, Histrionic, Paranoid, Obsessive-Compulsive, Schizoid, Schizotypal, Masochistic, Sadistic, Depressive, Negativistic-Passive-Aggressive, Dependent, and other Personality Disorders!

Click on this link to purchase the e-book or the print edition:

https://www.amazon.com/dp/B00708SLRE

NEW!!! "How to Divorce a Narcissist or a Psychopath"

Divorcing a narcissist or a psychopath is no easy or dangerless task. This book is no substitute for legal aid, though it does provide copious advice on anything from hiring an attorney, to domestic violence shelters, planning your getaway, involving the police, and obtaining restraining orders. Issues from court-mandated evaluation to custody are elaborated upon. The book describes the psychology of psychopathic narcissists, paranoids, bullies and stalkers and guides you through dozens of coping strategies and techniques, especially if you have shared children.

Click on this link now:

https://www.amazon.com/dp/B00759NMQ8

New!!! "How to Cope with Narcissistic and Psychopathic Abusers and Stalkers"

How to cope with stalkers, bullies, narcissists, psychopaths, and other abusers in the family, community, and workplace; how to navigate a system, which is often hostile to the victim: the courts, law enforcement (police), psychotherapists, evaluators, and social or welfare services; tips, advice, and information.

Click on this link now:

https://www.amazon.com/dp/B0080X5LYE

III. Video Lectures on DVDs

Purchase **3 DVDs** with 16 hours of video lectures on narcissists, psychopaths, and abuse in relationships – click on this link:

http://www.ccnow.com/cgi-local/cart.cgi?vaksam_DVD

Save 73$! Purchase the **3 DVDs** (16 hours of video lectures) + The Narcissism, Psychopathy and Abuse in Relationships Series of **SIXTEEN e-BOOKS** – click on this link:

http://www.ccnow.com/cgi-local/cart.cgi?vaksam_DVDSERIES

Purchase the **3 DVDs** (16 hours of video lectures) + the print book **"Malignant Self-love: Narcissism Revisited"** (tenth print edition) – click on this link:

http://www.ccnow.com/cgi-local/cart.cgi?vaksam_DVDPRINT

Free excerpts from the TENTTH, Revised Impression of "Malignant Self-love: Narcissism Revisited" are available as well as a **NEW EDITION of the Narcissism Book of Quotes**.

Click on this link to download the files:

http://www.narcissistic-abuse.com/freebooks.html

Additional Resources

Testimonials and Additional Resources

You can read Readers' Reviews at the Barnes and Noble Web page dedicated to "Malignant Self-love" – HERE:

http://search.barnesandnoble.com/bookSearch/isbnInquiry.asp?r=1&ISBN=9788023833843

Links to Therapist Directories, Psychological Tests, NPD Resources, Support Groups for narcissists and their victims, and Tutorials:

https://groups.yahoo.com/neo/groups/narcissisticabuse/conversations/messages/5458

Support groups for victims of narcissists and psychopaths (and one or two groups for narcissists)

http://dmoz.org/Health/Mental_Health/Disorders/Personality/Narcissistic/Support_Groups/